Vegetarian Diet Cookbook for Beginners

Respect Nature respect your body
quick and easy recipes
for a healthy life

Charlotte Evans

Additionally, the information in the following pages is intended only for informational purposes and should thus be thought of as universal. As befitting its nature, it is presented without assurance regarding its prolonged validity or interim quality. Trademarks that are mentioned are done without written consent and can in no way be considered an endorsement from the trademark holder.

Well-known American nutritionist Charlotte Evans was born in Buffalo NY in 1963 and dedicated many years of her life to the study of nutrition, graduating with honors in "Nutrition Science" from Stanford University in 1993.

Immediately after graduation, she began the working career that led her to collaborate for several years with renowned doctors in the field, during this period she was able to understand what are the difficulties that afflict all people who can not afford a normal diet.

For this reason, Evans decides to undertake the path that sees her realize the creation of easy recipe books for people with eating disorders, succeeding in making taste the main ingredient.

Table of content

—

INTRODUCTION

Although the word "plant-based" seems a bit new, the concept has been around for nearly 10,000 years. In fact, the Chinese began growing grains before domesticating animals more than 5,000 years ago, and that's how they sustained their population for centuries. Plants and vegetables are rich in great elements and
micronutrients that give our bodies
everything we need for a healthy, productive life. A plant-based eating routine supports and improves our bodies. Eating more plants is the first nutritional convention known to man to counteract the incessant diseases that assail our public. This is the origin of the term "plant-based diet," chosen to identify this eating pattern without being tied to any ethical or moral purpose. What is a plant-based diet? The idea is simple: you eat mainly plants or things that come from plants, such as seeds and grains. That being said, it is a fact that some people sometimes allow small portions of animal products in their plant-based diet, although it is recommended that they avoid them. You may be wondering what the difference is with veganism. The plant-based diet is different from veganism in the sense that vegans exclude all animal products from their diet without exception. This is a big difference! Veganism is a lifestyle that excludes meat and animal products (such as eggs, milk, honey) from one's diet. It's more like a "religion" where people don't eat those products for ethical reasons.
In principle, a plant-based diet has no particular ethical purpose, although more and more people are coming to this diet because they know it is more sustainable for our planet. By helping yourself you help the planet, what could be better?

BREAKFAST

Breakfast Bowl

Preparation Time: 5-15 minutes
Cooking Time: 25 minutes
Servings: 4
Ingredients:

- 1 cup brown quinoa, rinsed well
- • Salt to taste
- 3 tbsp plant-based yogurt
- ½ lime, juiced
- 2 tbsp chopped fresh cilantro
- 1 (5 oz) can black beans, drained and rinsed
- 3 tbsp tomato salsa
- ¼ small avocado, pitted, peeled, and sliced
- 2 radishes, shredded
- 1 tbsp pepitas (pumpkin seeds)

Directions:

1. Cook the quinoa with 2 cups of slightly salted water in a medium pot over medium heat or until the liquid absorbs, 15 minutes.
2. Spoon the quinoa into serving bowls and fluff with a fork.
3. In a small bowl, mix the yogurt, lime juice, cilantro, and salt. Divide this mixture on the quinoa and top with the beans, salsa, avocado, radishes, and pepitas.
4. Serve immediately.

Nutrition: Calories 131 Fats 3. 5g Carbs 20 Protein 6. 5g Corn Griddle

Cakes With Tofu Mayonnaise

Preparation Time: 5-15 minutes

Cooking Time: 35 minutes

Servings: 4

Ingredients:

- 1 tbsp flax seed powder + 3 tbsp water
- 1 cup water or as needed
- 2 cups yellow cornmeal
- 1 tsp salt
- 2 tsp baking powder
- 4 tbsp olive oil for frying
- 1 cup tofu mayonnaise for serving

Directions:

1. In a medium bowl, mix the flax seed powder with water and allow thickening for 5 minutes to form the flax egg.
2. Mix in the water and then whisk in the cornmeal, salt, and baking powder until soup texture forms but not watery.
3. Heat a quarter of the olive oil in a griddle pan and pour in a quarter of the batter. Cook until set and golden brown beneath, 3 minutes. Flip the cake and cook the other side until set and golden brown too.
4. Plate the cake and make three more with the remaining oil and batter.
5. Top the cakes with some tofu mayonnaise before serving

Nutrition: Calories 896 Fats 50. 7g Carbs 91. 6g Protein 17. 3g

Savory Breakfast Salad

Preparation Time: 15-30 minutes

Cooking Time: 20 minutes

Servings: 2

Ingredients:

- Sweet potato: 2 small
- Salt and pepper: 1 pinch
- Coconut oil: 1 tbsp
- Lemon juice: 3 tbsp
- Salt and pepper: 1 pinch each
- Extra virgin olive oil: 1 tbsp
- Mixed greens: 4 cups
- 4 tbsp Hummus
- Blueberries: 1 cup
- Ripe avocado: 1 medium
- Fresh chopped parsley
- Hemp seeds: 2 tbsp

Directions:

1. Take a large skillet and apply gentle heat
2. Add sweet potatoes, coat them with salt and pepper and pour some oil
3. Cook till sweet potatoes turns browns
4. Take a bowl and mix lemon juice, salt, and pepper
5. Add salad, sweet potatoes, and the serving together
6. Mix well and dress and serve

Nutrition: Carbs: 57. 6g Protein: 7. 5g Fats: 37. 6g Calories: 523 Kcal

Almond Plum Oats Overnight

Preparation Time: 15-30 minutes

Cooking Time: 10 minutes plus overnight

Servings: 2

Ingredients:

- Rolled oats: 60g
- Plums: 3 ripe and chopped
- Almond milk: 300ml
- Chia seeds: 1 tbsp
- Nutmeg: a pinch
- Vanilla extract: a few drops
- Whole almonds: 1 tbsp roughly chopped

Directions:

1. Add oats, nutmeg, vanilla extract, almond milk, and chia seeds to a bowl and mix well
2. Add in cubed plums and cover and place in the fridge for a night
3. Mix the oats well next morning and add into the serving bowl
4. Serve with your favorite toppings

Nutrition: Carbs: 24. 7g Protein: 9. 5g Fats: 10. 8g Calories: 248Kcal

High Protein Toast

Preparation Time: 15-30 minutes
Cooking Time: 15 minutes
Servings: 2
Ingredients:

- White bean: 1 drained and rinsed
- Cashew cream: ½ cup
- Miso paste: 1 ½ tbsp
- Toasted sesame oil: 1 tsp
- Sesame seeds: 1 tbsp
- Spring onion: 1 finely sliced
- Lemon: 1 half for the juice and half wedged to serve
- Rye bread: 4 slices toasted

Directions:

1. In a bowl add sesame oil, white beans, miso, cashew cream, and lemon juice and mash using a potato masher
2. Make a spread
3. Spread it on a toast and top with spring onions and sesame seeds
4. Serve with lemon wedges

Nutrition: Carbs: 44. 05 g Protein: 14. 05 g Fats: 9. 25 g Calories: 332 Kcal

Vegan Breakfast Hash

Preparation Time: 15-30 minutes

Cooking Time: 25 minutes

Servings: 4

Ingredients:

- Bell Pepper: 1
- Smoked Paprika: ½ tsp
- Potatoes: 3 medium
- Mushrooms: 8 oz
- Yellow Onion: 1
- Zucchini: 1
- Cumin Powder: ½ tsp
- Garlic Powder: ½ tsp
- Salt and Pepper: as per your taste
- Cooking oil: 2 tbsp (optional)

Directions:

1. Heat a large pan on medium flame, add oil and put the sliced potatoes
2. Cook the potatoes till they change color
3. Cut the rest of the vegetables and add all the spices
4. Cooked till veggies are soften

Nutrition: Carbs: 29. 7g Protein: 5. 5g Fats: 10g Calories: 217 Kcal

Vegan Muffins Breakfast Sandwich

Preparation Time: 15-30 minutes

Cooking Time: 20 minutes

Servings: 2

Ingredients:

- Romesco Sauce: 3-4 tablespoons
- Fresh baby spinach: ½ cup
- Tofu Scramble: 2
- Vegan English muffins: 2
- Avocado: ½ peeled and sliced

- Sliced fresh tomato: 1

Directions:

1. In the oven, toast English muffin
2. Half the muffin and spread romesco sauce
3. Paste spinach to one side, tailed by avocado slices
4. Have warm tofu followed by a tomato slice
5. Place the other muffin half onto to the preceding one

Nutrition: Carbs: 18g Protein: 12g Fats: 14g Calories: 276 Kcal

Almond Waffles With Cranberries

Preparation Time: 5-15 minutes
Cooking Time: 20 minutes
Servings: 4

Ingredients:

- 2 tbsp flax seed powder + 6 tbsp water
- 2/3 cup almond flour
- 2 ½ tsp baking powder
- A pinch salt
- 1 ½ cups almond milk
- 2 tbsp plant butter
- 1 cup fresh almond butter
- 2 tbsp pure maple syrup
- 1 tsp fresh lemon juice

Directions:

1. In a medium bowl, mix the flax seed powder with water and allow soaking for 5 minutes. • Add the almond flour, baking powder, salt, and almond milk.
2. Mix until well combined.
3. Preheat a waffle iron and brush with some plant butter.
4. Pour in a quarter cup of the batter, close the iron and cook until the waffles are

golden and crisp, 2 to 3 minutes.

5. Transfer the waffles to a plate and make more waffles using the same process and ingredient proportions.

6. Meanwhile, in a medium bowl, mix the almond butter with the maple syrup and lemon juice.

7. Serve the waffles, spread the top with the almond-lemon mixture, and serve.

Nutrition: Calories 533 Fats 53g Carbs 16. 7g Protein 1. 2g

Chickpea Omelet With Spinach And Mushrooms

Preparation Time: 5-15 minutes
Cooking Time: 25 minutes
Servings: 4
Ingredients:

- 1 cup chickpea flour
- ½ tsp onion powder
- ½ tsp garlic powder
- ¼ tsp white pepper
- ¼ tsp black pepper
- 1/3 cup nutritional yeast
- ½ tsp baking soda
- 1 small green bell pepper, deseeded and chopped
- 3 scallions, chopped
- 1 cup sautéed sliced white button mushrooms
- ½ cup chopped fresh spinach
- 1 cup halved cherry tomatoes for serving
- 1 tbsp fresh parsley leaves

Directions:

1. In a medium bowl, mix the chickpea flour, onion powder, garlic powder, white pepper, black pepper, nutritional

yeast, and baking soda until well combined.

2. Heat a medium skillet over medium heat and add a quarter of the batter.

3. Swirl the pan to spread the batter across the pan.

4. Scatter a quarter each of the bell pepper, scallions, mushrooms, and spinach on top, and cook until the bottom part of the omelet sets and is golden brown, 1 to 2 minutes.

5. Carefully, flip the omelet and cook the other side until set and golden brown.

6. Transfer the omelet to a plate and make the remaining omelets using the remaining batter in the same proportions.

7. Serve the omelet with the tomatoes and garnish with the parsley leaves.

8. Serve.

Nutrition: Calories 147 Fats 1. 8g Carbs 21. 3g Protein 11. 6g

Sweet Coconut Raspberry Pancakes

Preparation Time: 5-15 minutes
Cooking Time: 25 minutes
Servings: 4
Ingredients:

- 2 tbsp flax seed powder + 6 tbsp water
- ½ cup of coconut milk
- ¼ cup fresh raspberries, mashed
- ½ cup oat flour
- 1 tsp baking soda
- A pinch salt
- 1 tbsp coconut sugar
- 2 tbsp pure date syrup
- ½ tsp cinnamon powder

- 2 tbsp unsweetened coconut flakes
- 2 tsp plant butter
- Fresh raspberries for garnishing

Directions:

1. In a medium bowl, mix the flax seed powder with the water and allow thickening for 5 minutes.
2. Mix in the coconut milk and raspberries.
3. Add the oat flour, baking soda, salt, coconut sugar, date syrup, and cinnamon powder.
4. Fold in the coconut flakes until well combined.
5. Working in batches, melt a quarter of the butter in a non-stick skillet and add ¼ cup of the batter.
6. Cook until set beneath and golden brown, 2 minutes.
7. Flip the pancake and cook on the other side until set and golden brown, 2 minutes.
8. Transfer to a plate and make the remaining pancakes using the rest of the ingredients in the same proportions.
9. Garnish the pancakes with some raspberries and serve warm!

Nutrition: Calories 412 Fats 28. 3g Carbs 33. 7g Protein 7. 6g

Blueberry French Toast Breakfast Muffins

Preparation Time: 20 minutes
Cooking Time: 25 minutes
Servings: 12
Ingredients:

- 1 cup unsweetened plant milk
- 1 tablespoon ground flaxseed

- 1 tablespoon almond meal
- 1 tablespoon maple syrup
- 1 teaspoon vanilla extract
- 1 teaspoon cinnamon
- 2 teaspoons nutritional yeast
- ¾th cup frozen blueberries
- 9 slices soft bread
- ¼th cup oats
- 1/3rd cup raw pecans
- ¼th cup of coconut sugar
- 3 tablespoons coconut butter, at room temperature
- 1/8th teaspoon sea salt
- 9 slices bread, each cut into 4

Directions:

1. Preheat your oven to 370°F and grease a muffin tin.
2. Pop to one side.
3. Find a medium bowl and add the flaxseeds, almond meal, nutritional yeast, maple syrup, milk, vanilla, and cinnamon.
4. Mix well using a fork then pop into the fridge.
5. Grab your food processor and add the topping ingredients (except the coconut butter.)
6. Whizz to combine.
7. Add the butter then whizz again.
8. Grab your muffin tin and add a teaspoon of the flax and cinnamon batter to the bottom of each space.
9. Add a square of the bread then top with 5-6 blueberries.
10. Sprinkle with 2 teaspoons of the crumble then top with another piece of bread.
11. Place 5-6 more blueberries over the bread, sprinkle with more of the topping then add the other piece of bread.
12. Add a tablespoon of the flax and cinnamon mixture over

the top and add a couple of blueberries on the top.

13. Pop into the oven and cook for 20-25 minutes until the top begins to brown.

14. Serve and enjoy.

Nutrition: calories 132 fat 5 carbs 14 protein 3

Greek Garbanzo Beans on Toast

Preparation Time: 25 minutes
Cooking Time: 5 minutes
Servings: 2
Ingredients:

- 2 tablespoons olive oil
- 3 small shallots, finely diced
- 2 large garlic cloves, finely diced
- ¼ teaspoon smoked paprika
- ½ teaspoon sweet paprika
- ½ teaspoon cinnamon
- ½ teaspoon salt
- ½-1 teaspoon sugar, to taste
- Black pepper, to taste
- 1 x 14 oz. can peel plum tomatoes
- 2 cups cooked garbanzo beans
- 4-6 slices of crusty bread, toasted
- Fresh parsley and dill
- Pitted Kalamata olives

Directions:

1. Pop a skillet over medium heat and add the oil.
2. Add the shallots to the pan and cook for five minutes.
3. Add the garlic and cook until ready then add the other spices to the pan.
4. Stir well then add the tomatoes.
5. Lower the heat and simmer on low until the sauce thickens.

6. Add the garbanzo beans and warm through.
7. Season with the sugar, salt, and pepper, then serve and enjoy.

Nutrition: calories 709 fat 12 carbs 23 protein 19

Easy Hummus Toast

Preparation Time: 10 minutes
Cooking Time: 10 minutes
Servings: 1
Ingredients:
- 2 slices sprouted wheat bread
- ¼ cup hummus
- 1 tablespoon hemp seeds
- 1 tablespoon roasted unsalted sunflower seeds

Directions:
1. Start by toasting your bread.

2. Top with the hummus and seeds then eat!

Nutrition: calories 316 fat 16 carbs 13 protein 18

No-Bake Chewy Granola Bars

Preparation Time: 10 minutes
Cooking Time: 10 minutes
Servings: 8
Ingredients:
- ¼ teaspoon cinnamon
- ¼ teaspoon salt
- ½ teaspoon cardamom
- ¼ cup of coconut oil
- 1 cup oats
- 1 teaspoon vanilla extract
- ½ cup raw almonds, sliced
- ¼ cup sunflower seeds
- ½ cup pumpkin seeds
- 1¼ teaspoon nutmeg
- 1 tbsp chia seeds

- ¼ cup honey
- 1 cup dried figs, chopped

Directions:

1. Line a 6" x 8" baking dish with parchment paper and pop to one side.
2. Grab a saucepan and add the salt, honey, oil, and spices.
3. Pop over medium heat and stir until it melts together.
4. Reduce the heat, add the oats, and stir.
5. Add the dried fruit, seeds, and nuts, and stir through again.
6. Cook for 10 minutes.
7. Remove from the heat and transfer the oat mixture to the pan.
8. Press down until it's packed firm.
9. Leave to cool completely then cut into 8 bars.
10. Serve and enjoy.

Nutrition: calories 308 fat 14 carbs 35 protein 6

Tasty Oatmeal and Carrot Cake

Preparation Time: 5 minutes
Cooking Time: 10 minutes
Servings: 2
Ingredients:

- 1 cup of water
- ½ teaspoon of cinnamon
- 1 cup of rolled oats
- Salt
- ¼ cup of raisins
- ½ cup of shredded carrots
- 1 cup of non-dairy milk
- ¼ teaspoon of allspice
- ½ teaspoon of vanilla extract

Toppings:

- ¼ cup of chopped walnuts
- 2 tablespoons of maple syrup

- 2 tablespoons of shredded coconut

Directions:

1. Put a small pot on low heat and bring the non-dairy milk, oats, and water to a simmer.
2. Now, add the carrots, vanilla extract, raisins, salt, cinnamon, and allspice.
3. You need to simmer all the ingredients, but do not forget to stir them.
4. You will know that they are ready when the liquid is fully absorbed into all the ingredients (in about 7-10 minutes).
5. Transfer the thickened dish to bowls.
6. You can top them with coconut or walnuts.
7. This nutritious bowl will allow you to kickstart your day.

Nutrition: calories 210 fat 11 carbs 42 protein 4

Avocado Toast with White Beans

Preparation Time: 5 minutes
Cooking Time: 6 minutes
Servings: 4
Ingredients:

- ½ cup canned white beans, drained and rinsed
- 2 teaspoons tahini paste
- 2 teaspoons lemon juice
- ½ teaspoon salt
- ½ avocado, peeled and pit removed
- 4 slices whole-grain bread, toasted
- ½ cup grape tomatoes, cut in half

Directions:

1. Grab a small bowl and add the beans, tahini, ½ the lemon juice, and ½ the salt.
2. Mash with a fork.
3. Take another bowl and add the avocado and the remaining lemon juice and salt.
4. Mash together.
5. Place your toast onto a flat surface and add the mashed beans, spreading well.
6. Top with the avocado and the sliced tomatoes then serve and enjoy.

Nutrition: calories 140 fat 5 carbs 13 protein 5

Oatmeal & Peanut Butter Breakfast Bar

Preparation Time: 10 minutes
Cooking Time: 0 minutes
Servings: 8
Ingredients:
- 1 ½ cups date, pit removed
- ½ cup peanut butter
- ½ cup old-fashioned rolled oats

Directions:
1. Grease a baking tin and pop to one side.
2. Grab your food processor, add the dates, and whizz until chopped.
3. Add the peanut butter and the oats and pulse.
4. Scoop into the baking tin then pop into the fridge or freezer until set.
5. Serve and enjoy.

Nutrition: calories 232 fat 9 carbs 32 protein 8

Chocolate Chip Banana Pancake

Preparation Time: 15 minutes

Cooking Time: 3 minutes

Servings: 6

Ingredients:

- 1 large ripe banana, mashed
- 2 tablespoons coconut sugar
- 3 tablespoons coconut oil, melted
- 1 cup of coconut milk
- 1 ½ cups whole wheat flour
- 1 teaspoon baking soda
- ½ cup vegan chocolate chips
- Olive oil, for frying

Directions:

1. Grab a large bowl and add the banana, sugar, oil, and milk.
2. Stir well.
3. Add the flour and baking soda and stir again until combined.
4. Add the chocolate chips and fold through then pop to one side.
5. Put a skillet over medium heat and add a drop of oil.
6. Pour ¼ of the batter into the pan and move the pan to cover.
7. Cook for 3 minutes then flip and cook on the other side.
8. Repeat with the remaining pancakes then serve and enjoy.

Nutrition: calories 105 fat 13 carbs 23 protein 5

Avocado and 'Sausage' Breakfast Sandwich

Preparation Time: 15 minutes

Cooking Time: 10 minutes

Servings: 1

Ingredients:

- 1 vegan sausage patty
- 1 cup kale, chopped
- 2 teaspoons extra virgin olive oil
- 1 tablespoon pepitas
- Salt and pepper, to taste
- 1 tablespoon vegan mayo
- 1/8 teaspoon chipotle powder
- 1 teaspoon jalapeno chopped
- 1 English muffin, toasted
- ¼ avocado, sliced

Directions:

1. Place a sauté pan over high heat and add a drop of oil.
2. Add the vegan patty and cook for 2 minutes.
3. Flip the patty then add the kale and pepitas.
4. Season well then cook for another few minutes until the patty is cooked.
5. Find a small bowl and add the mayo, chipotle powder, and the jalapeno.
6. Stir well to combine.
7. Place the muffin onto a flat surface, spread with the spicy mayo then top with the patty.
8. Add the sliced avocado then serve and enjoy.

Nutrition: calories 573 fat 23 carbs 36 protein 21

Cinnamon Rolls with Cashew Frosting

Preparation Time: 25 minutes

Cooking Time: 25 minutes

Servings: 12

Ingredients:

- 3 tablespoons vegan butter
- ¾ cup unsweetened almond milk
- ½ teaspoon salt
- 3 tablespoons caster sugar
- 1 teaspoon vanilla extract
- ½ cup pumpkin puree
- 3 cups all-purpose flour
- 2 ¼ teaspoons dried active yeast
- 3 tablespoons softened vegan butter
- 3 tablespoons brown sugar
- ½ teaspoon cinnamon
- ½ cup cashews
- ½ cup icing sugar
- 1 teaspoon vanilla extract
- 2/3 cup almond milk

Directions:

1. Soak the cashews for 1 hour in boiling water.
2. Grease a baking sheet and pop to one side.
3. Find a small bowl, add the butter, and pop into the microwave to melt.
4. Add the sugar and stir well then set aside to cool.
5. Grab a large bowl and add the flour, salt, and yeast.
6. Stir well to mix.
7. Place the cooled butter into a jug, add the pumpkin puree, vanilla, and almond milk.
8. Stir well together.
9. Pour the wet ingredients into the dry and stir well to combine.
10. Tip onto a flat surface and knead for 5 minutes, adding extra flour as needed to avoid sticking.
11. Pop back into the bowl, cover with plastic wrap, and pop into the fridge overnight.
12. Remove the dough from the fridge and punch down with your fingers.

13. Using a rolling pin, roll to form an 18" rectangle then spread with butter.

14. Find a small bowl and add the sugar and cinnamon.

15. Mix well then sprinkle with the butter.

16. Roll the dough into a large sausage then slice into sections.

17. Place onto the greased baking sheet and leave in a dark place to rise for one hour.

18. Preheat the oven to 350°F.

19. Drain the cashews and put them to your blender.

20. Whizz until smooth.

21. Add the sugar and the vanilla then whizz again.

22. Add the almond milk until it reaches your desired consistency.

23. Pop into the oven and bake for 20 minutes until golden.

24. Pour the glaze over the top then serve and enjoy.

Nutrition: calories 243 fat 9 carbs 34 protein 4

Banana Bread Shake With Walnut Milk

Preparation time: 5 minutes
Cooking time: 0 minute
Servings: 2
Ingredients:
- 2 cups sliced frozen bananas
- 3 cups walnut milk
- 1/8 teaspoon grated nutmeg
- 1 tablespoon maple syrup
- 1 teaspoon ground cinnamon
- 1/2 teaspoon vanilla extract, unsweetened
- 2 tablespoons cacao nibs

Directions:
1. Place all the ingredients in the order in a food processor

or blender and then pulse for 2 to 3 minutes at high speed until smooth.
2. Pour the smoothie into two glasses and then serve.

Nutrition: Calories: 199 Fat: 9,1g Carbohydrates: 1.5g Protein: 8g

Strawberry, Banana and Coconut Shake

Preparation time: 5 minutes
Cooking time: 0 minute
Servings: 1
Ingredients:

- 1 tablespoon coconut flakes
- 1 1/2 cups frozen banana slices
- 8 strawberries, sliced
- 1/2 cup coconut milk, unsweetened
- 1/4 cup strawberries for topping

Directions:

1. Place all the ingredients in the order in a food processor or blender, except for topping and then pulse for 2 to 3 minutes at high speed until smooth.
2. Pour the smoothie into a glass and then serve.

Nutrition: Calories: 219 Fat: 10.1g Carbohydrates: 1.5g Protein: 7.9g

Peanut Butter and Mocha Smoothie

Preparation time: 5 minutes
Cooking time: 0 minute
Servings: 1
Ingredients:

- 1 frozen banana, chopped
- 1 scoop of chocolate protein powder

- 2 tablespoons rolled oats
- 1/8 teaspoon sea salt
- ¼ teaspoon vanilla extract, unsweetened
- 1 teaspoon cocoa powder, unsweetened
- 2 tablespoons peanut butter
- 1 shot of espresso
- ½ cup almond milk, unsweetened

Directions:

1. Place all the ingredients in the order in a food processor or blender and then pulse for 2 to 3 minutes at high speed until smooth.
2. Pour the smoothie into a glass and then serve.

Nutrition: Calories: 215 Fat: 10.8g Carbohydrates: 1.3g Protein: 7.9g

Ginger and Greens Smoothie

Preparation time: 5 minutes
Cooking time: 0 minute
Servings: 1
Ingredients:
- 1 frozen banana
- 2 cups baby spinach
- 2-inch piece of ginger, peeled, chopped
- ¼ teaspoon cinnamon
- ¼ teaspoon vanilla extract, unsweetened
- 1/8 teaspoon salt
- 1 scoop vanilla protein powder
- 1/8 teaspoon cayenne pepper
- 2 tablespoons lemon juice
- 1 cup of orange juice

Directions:
1. Place all the ingredients in the order in a food processor or blender and then pulse for 2 to 3 minutes at high speed until smooth.
2. Pour the smoothie into a glass and then serve.

Nutrition: Calories: 221 Fat: 10.9g Carbohydrates: 1.7g Protein: 7.9g

Sweet Potato Smoothie

Preparation time: 5 minutes
Cooking time: 0 minute
Servings: 1
Ingredients:

- 1/2 cup frozen zucchini pieces
- 1 cup cubed cooked sweet potato, frozen
- 1/2 frozen banana
- 1/2 teaspoon sea salt
- 1/2 teaspoon cinnamon
- 1 scoop of vanilla protein powder
- 1/4 teaspoon nutmeg
- 1 tablespoon almond butter
- 1 1/2 cups almond milk, unsweetened

Directions:

1. Place all the ingredients in the order in a food processor or blender and then pulse for 2 to 3 minutes at high speed until smooth.
2. Pour the smoothie into a glass and then serve.

Nutrition: Calories: 219 Fat: 10.1g Carbohydrates: 1.5g Protein: 7.9g

Chickpeas On Toast

Preparation time: 5 minutes
Cooking time: 15 minutes
Servings: 6
Ingredients:

- 14-oz cooked chickpeas
- 1 cup baby spinach
- 1/2 cup chopped white onion
- 1 cup crushed tomatoes
- ½ teaspoon minced garlic

- ¼ teaspoon ground black pepper
- 1/2 teaspoon brown sugar
- 1 teaspoon smoked paprika powder
- 1/3 teaspoon sea salt
- 1 tablespoon olive oil
- 6 slices of gluten-free bread, toasted

Directions:

1. Take a frying pan, place it over medium heat, add oil and when hot, add onion and cook for 2 minutes.
2. Then stir in garlic, cook for 30 seconds until fragrant, stir in paprika and continue cooking for 10 seconds.
3. Add tomatoes, stir, bring the mixture to simmer, season with black pepper, sugar, and salt and then stir in chickpeas.
4. Sir, in spinach, cook for 2 minutes until leaves have wilted, then remove the pan from heat and taste to adjust seasoning.
5. Serve cooked chickpeas on toasted bread

Nutrition: Calories: 228Fat: 10.1g Carbohydrates: 1.4g Protein: 7.9g

Chickpea Omelet

Preparation time: 5 minutes
Cooking time: 10 minutes
Servings: 1
Ingredients:

- 3 Tablespoon chickpea flour
- 1 small white onion, peeled, diced
- ½ teaspoon black salt
- 2 tablespoons chopped the dill
- 2 tablespoons chopped basil

- 1/8 teaspoon ground black pepper
- 2 Tablespoon olive oil
- 8 Tablespoon water

Directions:

1. Take a bowl, add flour in it along with salt and black pepper, stir until mixed, and then whisk in water until creamy.
2. Take a skillet pan, place it over medium heat, add 1 tablespoon oil and when hot, add onion and cook for 4 minutes until cooked.
3. Add onion to omelet mixture and then stir until combined.
4. Add remaining oil into the pan, pour in prepared batter, spread evenly, and cook for 3 minutes per side until cooked.
5. Serve omelet with bread.

Nutrition: Calories: 228Fat: 11.1g Carbohydrates: 1.4g Protein: 7.9g

Pancake

Preparation time: 10 minutes
Cooking time: 18 minutes
Servings: 4
Ingredients:
Dry Ingredients:

- 1 cup buckwheat flour
- 1/8 teaspoon salt
- ½ teaspoon gluten-free baking powder
- ½ teaspoon baking soda

Wet Ingredients:

- 1 tablespoon almond butter
- 2 tablespoon maple syrup
- 1 tablespoon lime juice
- 1 cup coconut milk, unsweetened

Directions:

1. Take a medium bowl, add all the dry ingredients and stir until mixed.
2. Take another bowl, place all the wet ingredients, whisk until combined, and then gradually whisk in dry ingredients mixture until smooth and incorporated.
3. Take a frying pan, place it over medium heat, add 2 teaspoons oil and when hot, drop in batter and cook for 3 minutes per side until cooked and lightly browned.
4. Serve pancakes and fruits and maple syrup.

Nutrition: Calories: 231 Fat: 10.1g Carbohydrates: 2.4g Protein: 7.9g

Apple Pancakes

Preparation Time: 15 minutes
Cooking Time: 4 minutes
Servings: 4
Ingredients:

- 1 cup whole-wheat flour
- ¾ tsp. ground cinnamon, divided
- ¼ tsp. baking soda
- 1 tsp. baking powder Pinch salt
- 1 egg
- ¾ cup ricotta cheese
- 1 cup buttermilk
- 1 tsp. vanilla extract
- 1 tbsp. sugar and 1 tsp. sugar, divided
- 1 apple, sliced into rings
- 4 tsp. butter
- 4 tsp. walnut oil

Directions:

1. In a bowl, mix the flour, ½ teaspoon cinnamon, baking soda, baking powder and salt.

2. In another bowl, beat the eggs and stir in the cheese, milk, vanilla and 1 tablespoon sugar.
3. Gradually add the second bowl to the first one.
4. Mix well. Combine the remaining cinnamon and 1 teaspoon sugar in a separate dish.
5. Coat each apple ring with this mixture.
6. Pour the butter and oil in a pan over medium heat.
7. Add the apples and pour the batter around the apple.
8. Cook for 2 minutes.
9. Flip and cook for another 2 minutes.

Nutrition: Calories: 218Fat: 11.1g Carbohydrates: 1.4g Protein: 9.1g

Quinoa Black Beans Breakfast Bowl

Preparation Time: 15 Minutes
Cooking Time: 25 Minutes
Servings: 1
Ingredients:

- 1/4 cup brown quinoa, rinsed well
- Salt to taste
- 1 tbsp plant-based yogurt
- ½ lime, juiced
- 1 tbsp chopped fresh cilantro
- 1 (5 oz) can black beans, drained and rinsed
- 1 tbsp tomato salsa
- ¼ small avocado, pitted, peeled, and sliced
- 1 radish, shredded
- 1/4 tbsp pepitas (pumpkin seeds)

Directions:

1. Cook the quinoa with 2 cups of slightly salted water in a

medium pot over medium heat or until the liquid absorbs, 15 minutes.

2. Spoon the quinoa into serving bowls and fluff with a fork.

3. In a small bowl, mix the yogurt, lime juice, cilantro, and salt.

4. Divide this mixture on the quinoa and top with beans, salsa, avocado, radishes, and pepitas.

5. Serve immediately.

Nutrition: Calories: 131 Fats: 3.5g Carbs: 20g Proteins: 6.5g

Roasted Broccoli

Preparation Time: 10 Minutes
Cooking Time: 8 Minutes
Servings: 2
Ingredients:
- ¼ tsp. Masala
- ½ tsp. red chili powder
- ½ tsp. salt
- ¼ tsp. turmeric powder
- 1 tbsp. chickpea flour
- 2 tbsp. yogurt
- 1-pound broccoli

Direction:
1. Cut the broccoli into florets.
2. Immerse in a bowl of water with two teaspoons of salt for at least half an hour to remove impurities.
3. Remove the broccoli florets from the water and let them drain.
4. Clean thoroughly.
5. Mix all the other shopping lists: to make a marinade.
6. Stir the broccoli flowers into the marinade.
7. Cover and let cool for 15-30 minutes.
8. Air frying. Preheat the Instant Crisp Air Fryer to 390 degrees.
9. Put the marinated broccoli flowers in the deep fryer, close the lid of the air fryer, set the temperature to 350 ° F and set the time to 10 minutes.
10. The flowers will be crunchy when cooked.

Nutrition: Calories: 96 Fat: 1.3g Protein: 7g Sugar: 4.5g

Buffalo Cauliflower

Preparation Time: 5 Minutes
Cooking Time: 15 Minutes
Servings: 2
Instructions:
Cauliflower:
- 1 C. panko breadcrumbs
- 1 tsp. salt
- 4 C. cauliflower florets

Buffalo Coating:
- ¼ C. Vegan Buffalo sauce
- ¼ C. melted vegan butter

Direction:
1. Melt the butter in the microwave and whisk in the buffalo sauce.
2. Dip each cauliflower floret into the buffalo mixture, making sure it is well coated.
3. Keep a bowl until the flower drips.
4. Mix the breadcrumbs with the salt.
5. Air frying.
6. Drag the flowers dipped in breadcrumbs and place them in the Instant Crisp Air Fryer.
7. Lock the lid of the air fryer.
8. Set the temperature to 350 ° F and the time to 15 minutes.
9. When they are lightly browned, they are ready to eat!
10.   Serve with your favorite keto sauce!

Nutrition: Calories: 194 Fat: 17g Protein: 10g Sugar:

Zucchini Parmesan Chips

Preparation Time: 10 Minutes
Cooking Time: 8 Minutes
Servings: 10
Ingredients:
- ½ tsp. paprika
- ½ C. grated parmesan cheese
- ½ C. Italian breadcrumbs
- One lightly beaten egg
- Two thinly sliced zucchinis

Direction:
1. Use a very sharp knife or mandolin slicer to slice the zucchini as thin as possible.
2. Eliminate extra moisture.

3. Beat the egg with a pinch of pepper and salt and a little water.
4. Combine paprika, cheese and breadcrumbs in a bowl.
5. Dip the courgette slices in the egg mixture and then in the breadcrumb mixture.
6. Press gently to coat.
7. Air frying.
8. With cooking spray olive oil, courgette slices covered in mist.
9. Put it in your Instant Crisp Air Fryer in a single layer.
10. Lock the lid of the air fryer.
11. Set the temperature to 350 ° F and set the time to 8 minutes.
12. Sprinkle with salt and serve with the sauce.

Nutrition: Calories: 211 Fat: 16g Protein: 8g Sugar: 0g

Cauliflower Fritters

Preparation Time: 10 Minutes
Cooking Time: 7 Minutes
Servings: 8
Ingredients:
- ½ C. chopped parsley
- 1 C. Italian breadcrumbs
- 1/3 C. shredded mozzarella cheese
- 1/3 C. shredded sharp cheddar cheese
- One egg
- Two minced garlic cloves
- Three chopped scallions
- One head of cauliflower

Direction:
1. Cut the cauliflower into florets.
2. Wash well and pat dry.
3. Place in a food processor and blend for 20-30 seconds until it looks like rice.
4. Place the cauliflower rice in a bowl and mix with pepper, salt, eggs, cheese, breadcrumbs, garlic and shallots.
5. With your hands, form 15 meatballs of the mixture and add more breadcrumbs if necessary.
6. Air frying.
7. With olive oil, spritz the meatballs and place them in your Instant Crisp air fryer in a single layer.
8. Lock the lid of the air fryer.
9. Set the temperature to 390 ° F and set the time to 7

minutes, turning after 7 minutes.

Nutrition: Calories: 209 Fat: 17g Protein: 6g Sugar: 0.5

Blueberry Smoothie with Lemon

Preparation Time: 5 minutes
Cooking time: 0 minute
Servings: 1
Ingredients:
- 1 1/2 cups frozen blueberries
- 1/2 frozen banana
- 1 tablespoon chia seeds
- 3 tablespoon lemon juice
- 1 teaspoon lemon zest
- 1 1/2 teaspoon cinnamon
- 1 1/2 cups almond milk, unsweetened
- 1 scoop of vanilla protein powder

Direction:
1. Put the whole shopping list: in the order in a food processor or a blender and then blend for 2 or 3 minutes on high speed until smooth.
2. Pour the smoothie into a glass and serve.

Nutrition: Calories: 317 Cal Fat: 4 g Carbs: 67 g Protein: 6 g Fiber: 9 g

Guacamole

Preparation Time: 15 minutes
Cooking Time: 5 minutes
Servings: 4
Ingredients:
- Avocados: 3 ripe
- Fresh jalapeño chilies: 1 finely chopped
- Red onion: ¼ finely chopped
- Tomatoes: 2 small diced
- Garlic: ½ crushed
- Lime juice:2 tbsp
- Coriander: ¼ cup finely chopped
- Sea salt: 1 tsp
- Plain tortilla chips to serve

Direction:
1. How To Cook Take a bowl and add onion, chilies, garlic and lime juice
2. Add salt from the top, mix and leave for 5 minutes
3. Add the remaining ingredient and mash using a fork
4. Add avocados, mix and serve with plain tortilla chips

Nutrition: Amount Per Serving Carbs: 21.7 g Protein: 5.2 g Fats: 7.1 g Calories: 256 Kcal

High Protein Toast

Preparation Time: 15 minutes
Cooking Time:
Servings: 2
Ingredients:
- White bean: 1 drained and rinsed
- Cashew cream: ½ cup
- Miso paste: 1 ½ tbsp
- Toasted sesame oil: 1 tsp
- Sesame seeds: 1 tbsp
- Spring onion: 1 finely sliced
- Lemon:1 half for the juice and half wedged to serve
- Rye bread: 4 slices toasted

Direction:
1. How To Cook In a bowl add sesame oil, white beans, miso, cashew cream, and lemon juice and mash using a potato masher
2. Make a spread

3. Spread it on a toast and top with spring onions and sesame seeds
4. Serve with lemon wedges

Nutrition: Amount Per Serving Carbs: 44.05 g Protein: 14.05 g Fats: 9.25 g Calories: 332 Kcal

Hummus Carrot Sandwich

Preparation Time: 25 minutes
Cooking time:
Servings: 2
Ingredients:
- Chickpeas: 1 cup can drain and rinsed
- Tomato: 1 small sliced
- Cucumber: 1 sliced
- Avocado: 1 sliced
- Cumin: 1 tsp
- Carrot: 1 cup diced
- Maple syrup: 1 tsp
- Tahini: 3 tbsp
- Garlic: 1 clove
- Lemon: 2 tbsp
- Extra-virgin olive oil: 2 tbsp
- Salt: as per your need

- Bread slices: 4

Direction:
1. How To Cook Add carrot to the boiling hot water and boil for 15 minutes
2. Blend boiled carrots, maple syrup, cumin, chickpeas, tahini, olive oil, salt, and garlic together in a blender
3. Add in lemon juice and mix
4. Add to the serving bowl and you can refrigerate for up to 5 days
5. In between two bread slices, spread hummus and place 2-3 slices of cucumber, avocado, and tomato and serve

Nutrition: Amount Per Serving Carbs: 53.15 g Protein: 14.1 g Fats: 27.5 g Calories: 490 Kcal

Overnight Oats

Preparation Time: 15 minutes plus overnight
Cooking Time: 0 minutes
Servings: 6
Ingredients:
- Cinnamon: a pinch
- Almond milk: 600ml
- Porridge oats: 320g
- Maple syrup: 1 tbsp
- Pumpkin seeds 1 tbsp
- Chia seeds: 1 tbsp

Direction:
1. How To Cook Add all the ingredients to the bowl and combine well
2. Cover the bowl and place it in the fridge overnight
3. Pour more milk in the morning
4. Serve with your favorite toppings

Nutrition: Amount Per Serving Carbs: 32.3 g Protein: 10.2 g Fats: 12.7 g Calories: 298 Kcal

Savory Breakfast Salad

Preparation Time: 20 minutes
Cooking Time: 5/10 minutes
Servings: 2
Ingredients:
For the sweet potatoes:
- Sweet potato: 2 small
- Salt and pepper: 1 pinch
- Coconut oil:1 tbsp

For the Dressing:

- Lemon juice: 3 tbsp
- Salt and pepper: 1 pinch each
- Extra virgin olive oil:1 tbsp

For the Salad:
- Mixed greens: 4 cups

For Serving:
- Hummus: 4 tbsp
- Blueberries: 1 cup
- Ripe avocado: 1 medium
- Fresh chopped parsley
- Hemp seeds: 2 tbsp

Direction:
1. How To Cook Take a large skillet and apply gentle heat
2. Add sweet potatoes, coat them with salt and pepper and pour some oil
3. Cook till sweet potatoes turns browns
4. Take a bowl and mix lemon juice, salt, and pepper
5. Add salad, sweet potatoes, and the serving together
6. Mix well and dress and serve

Nutrition: Amount Per Serving Carbs: 57.6g Protein: 7.5g Fats: 37.6g Calories: 523 Kcal

Sweet Pomegranate Porridge

Preparation Time: 5 minutes
Cooking Time: 20 minutes
Servings: 4
Ingredients:
- 2 Cups Oats
- 1 ½ Cups Water
- 1 ½ Cups Pomegranate Juice
- 2 Tablespoons Pomegranate Molasses

Directions:
1. Pour all ingredients into the instant pot and mix well.
2. Seal the lid, and cook on high pressure for four minutes.
3. Use a quick release, and serve warm.

Nutrition: Calories: 177 Fat: 6g Carbs: 23g Protein: 8g

Apple Oatmeal

Preparation Time: 5 minutes
Cooking Time: 20 minutes
Servings: 4
Ingredients:
- ¼ Teaspoon Sea Salt
- 1 Cup Cashew Milk

- 1 Cup Strawberries, Halved & Fresh
- 1 Tablespoon Brown Sugar
- 2 Cups Apples, Diced
- 3 Cups Water
- ¼ Teaspoon Coconut Oil
- ½ Cup Steel Cut Oats

Directions:
1. Start by greasing your instant pot with oil, and add everything to it except for the milk and berries.
2. Lock the lid and cook on high pressure for ten minutes.
3. Allow for a natural pressure release, and then add in your milk and strawberries.
4. Mix well, and serve warm.

Nutrition: Calories: 435 Fat: 7g Carbs: 34g Protein: 8g

Breakfast Cookies

Preparation Time: 10 minutes
Cooking Time: 6 minutes
Servings: 24-32
Ingredients:
Dry Ingredients:
- ½ teaspoon baking powder
- 2 cups rolled oats
- ½ teaspoon baking soda

Wet Ingredients:
- 1 teaspoon pure vanilla extract
- 2 flax eggs (2 tablespoons ground flaxseed and around 6 tablespoons of water, mix and put aside for 15 minutes)
- 2 tablespoons melted coconut oil
- 2 tablespoons pure maple syrup
- ½ cup natural creamy peanut butter
- 2 ripe bananas
- Add-in Ingredients:
- ½ cup finely chopped walnuts
- ½ cup raisins

Optional Topping:
- 2 tablespoons chopped walnuts
- 2 tablespoons raisins

Directions:
1. Preheat the oven to 325°F, and then use parchment paper to line a baking sheet and put aside.
2. Add the bananas in a large bowl, and then use a fork to mash them until smooth. Add in the other wet ingredients

and mix until well incorporated.

3. Add the dry ingredients and then use a rubber spatula to stir and fold them into the dry ingredients until well mixed.
4. Stir in the walnuts and raisins.
5. Scoop the cookie dough onto the prepared baking sheet making sure that you leave adequate space between the cookies.
6. Bake in the preheated oven for around 12 minutes.
7. Once ready, let the cookies cool on the baking sheet for around 10 minutes.
8. Lift the cookies carefully from the baking sheet onto a cooling rack to further cool.
9. Store the cookies in an airtight container in the fridge or at room temperature for up to one week.

Nutrition: Calories: 565 Fat: 6g Carbs: 32g Protein: 8g

Vegan Breakfast Biscuits

Preparation Time: 10 minutes
Cooking Time: 10 min
Servings: 6
Ingredients:
- cups Almond Flour - quantity not mentioned
- 1 tbsp Baking Powder
- ¼ teaspoon Salt
- ½ teaspoon Onion Powder
- ½ cup Coconut Milk
- ¼ cup Nutritional Yeast
- 2 tbsp Ground Flax Seeds
- ¼ cup Olive Oil

Directions:
1. Preheat oven to 450°F.
2. Whisk together all ingredients in a bowl.
3. Divide the batter into a pre-greased muffin tin.
4. Bake for 10 minutes.

Nutrition: Calories: 432 Fat: 5g Carbs: 13g Protein: 8g

Nutrition: Calories: 129 Fat: 1.1g
Carbs: 21.5g Protein: 7.9g

Orange French Toast

Preparation Time: 5 minutes
Cooking Time: 30 minutes
Servings: 8
Ingredients:
- 2 cups of plant milk (unflavored)
- Four tablespoon maple syrup
- 11/2 tablespoon cinnamon
- Salt (optional)
- 1 cup flour (almond)
- 1 tablespoon orange zest
- 8 bread slices

Directions:
1. Turn the oven and heat to 400°F afterwards.
2. In a cup, add ingredients and whisk until the batter is smooth.
3. Dip each piece of bread into the paste and permit to soak for a couple of seconds.
4. Put in the pan, and cook until lightly browned.
5. Put the toast on the cookie sheet and bake for ten to fifteen minutes in the oven, until it is crispy.

LUNCH

Basil Spaghetti Pasta

Preparation Time: 05 minutes
Cooking Time: 05 minutes
Servings: 2
Ingredients:
- ½ teaspoon garlic powder
- 1 cup spaghetti
- 2 large eggs
- ¼ cup grated Parmesan cheese
- Freshly cracked pepper
- Salt and pepper to taste
- Handful fresh basil
- Enough water

Directions:
1. In a medium bowl, whisk together the eggs, 1/2 cup of the Parmesan cheese, and a generous dose of freshly cracked pepper.
2. Add spaghetti, water, basil, garlic powder, pepper, and salt to Instant Pot.
3. Place lid on Instant Pot and lock into place to seal.
4. Pressure Cook on High Pressure for 4 minutes.
5. Use Quick Pressure Release.
6. Pour the eggs and Parmesan mixture over the hot pasta.

Nutrition: Calories216, Total Fat 2. 3g, Saturated Fat 0. 7g, Cholesterol 49mg, Sodium 160mg, Total Carbohydrate 36g, Dietary Fiber 0. 1g, Total Sugars 0. 4g, Protein 12. 2g

Parsley Hummus Pasta

Preparation Time: 10 minutes
Cookng Time: 10 minutes
Serving: 2
Ingredients:
- ½ cup chickpeas
- 1/8 cup coconut oil
- ½ fresh lemon
- 1/8 cup tahini
- ½ teaspoon garlic powder
- 1/8 teaspoon cumin
- 1/4 teaspoon salt
- 1 green onion
- 1/8 bunch fresh parsley, or to taste
- 1 cup pasta
- Enough water

Directions:
1. Drain the chickpeas and add them to a food processor along with the coconut oil, juice from the lemon, tahini,

garlic powder, cumin, and salt.

2. Pulse the ingredients, adding a small amount of water if needed to keep it moving, until the hummus is smooth.
3. Slice the green onion (both white and green ends) and pull the parsley leaves from the stems.
4. Add the green onion and parsley to the hummus in the food processor and process again until only small flecks of green remain.
5. Taste the hummus and adjust the salt, lemon, or garlic if needed.
6. Add pasta, water into Instant Pot.
7. Place the lid on the pot and lock it into place to seal.
8. Pressure Cook on High Pressure for 4 minutes.
9. Use Quick Pressure Release.
10. In Sauté mode add hummus to pasta.
11. When it mixes, turn off the switch of Instant Pot.
12. Serve and enjoy.

Nutrition: Calories 582, Total Fat 26. 3g, Saturated Fat 13. 5g, Cholesterol 47mg, Sodium 338mg, Total Carbohydrate 71g, Dietary Fiber 10. 8g, Total Sugars 6. 1g, Protein 19. 9g

Creamy Spinach Artichoke Pasta

Preparation Time: 05 minutes
Cooking Time: 05 minutes
Servings: 2
Ingredients:
- 1 tablespoon butter
- ¼ teaspoon garlic powder
- 1 cup vegetable broth
- 1 cup of coconut milk
- ¼ teaspoon salt
- Freshly cracked pepper
- ½ cup pasta
- 1/4 cup fresh baby spinach
- ½ cup quartered artichoke hearts
- 1/8 cup grated Parmesan cheese

Direction:
1. In the Instant Pot, hit —Sauté, add butter when it melts, add garlic powder just until it's tender and fragrant.

2. Add the vegetable broth, coconut milk, salt, some freshly cracked pepper, and pasta.
3. Place
4. the lid on the pot and lock it into place to seal.
5. Pressure Cook on High Pressure for 4minutes.
6. Use Quick Pressure Release.
7. Add the spinach, a handful at a time, to the hot pasta and toss it in the pasta until it wilts into
8. Instant Pot in Sauté mode.
9. Stir the chopped artichoke hearts into the pasta.
10.   Sprinkle grated
11. Parmesan over the pasta, then stir slightly to incorporate the Parmesan.
12. Top with an additional Parmesan then serve.

Nutrition: Calories 457, Total Fat 36. 2g, Saturated Fat 29. 6g, Cholesterol 40mg, Sodium 779mg, Total Carbohydrate 27. 6g, Dietary Fiber 4g, Total Sugars 4. 7g, Protein 10. 3g

Easy Spinach Ricotta Pasta

Preparation Time: 05 minutes
Cooking Time: 10 minutes
Servings: 2
Ingredients:
- ½ cup pasta
- 1 cup vegetable broth
- 1/2 lb. uncooked tagliatelle
- 1 tablespoon coconut oil
- ½ teaspoon garlic powder
- ¼ cup almond milk
- ½ cup whole milk ricotta
- 1/8 teaspoon salt
- Freshly cracked pepper
- ¼ cup chopped spinach

Directions:
1. Add the vegetable broth, tagliatelle, spinach, salt, some freshly cracked pepper, and the pasta.
2. Place lid on Instant Pot and lock into place to seal.
3. Pressure Cook on High Pressure for 4 minutes.
4. Use Quick Pressure Release.
5. Prepare the ricotta sauce.
6. Mince the garlic and add it to a large skillet with coconut oil.

7. Cook over Medium-Low heat for 1-2 minutes, or just until soft and fragrant (but not browned).
8. Add the almond milk and ricotta, then stir until relatively smooth (the ricotta may be slightly grainy).
9. Allow the sauce to heat through and come to a low simmer.
10. The sauce will thicken slightly as it simmers.
11. Once it's thick enough to coat the spoon (3-5 minutes), season with salt and pepper.
12. Add the cooked and drained pasta to the sauce and toss to coat.
13. If the sauce becomes too thick or dry, add a small amount of the reserved pasta cooking water.
14. Serve warm.

Nutrition: Calories277, Total Fat 18. 9g, Saturated Fat 15. 2g, Cholesterol 16mg, Sodium 191mg,

Total Roasted Red Pepper Pasta

Preparation Time: 05 minutes
Cooking Time: 05 minutes
Servings: 2
Ingredients:
- 2 cups vegetable broth
- ½ cup spaghetti
- 1 small onion
- ½ teaspoon garlic minced
- ½ cup roasted red peppers
- ½ cup roasted diced tomatoes
- ¼ tablespoon dried mint
- 1/8 teaspoon crushed red pepper
- Freshly cracked black pepper
- ½ cup goat cheese

Directions:
1. In an Instant Pot, combine the vegetable broth, onion, garlic, red pepper slices, diced tomatoes, mint, crushed red pepper, and some freshly cracked black pepper.
2. Stir these ingredients to combine.
3. Add spaghetti to the Instant Pot.
4. Place lid on Instant Pot and lock into place to seal.

5. Pressure Cook on High Pressure for 4 minutes.
6. Use Quick Pressure Release.
7. Divide the goat cheese into tablespoon-sized pieces, then add them to the Instant Pot.
8. Stir the pasta until the cheese melts in and creates a smooth sauce.
9. Serve hot.

Nutrition: Calories198, Total Fat 4. 9g, Saturated Fat 2. 2g, Cholesterol 31mg, Sodium 909mg, Total Carbohydrate 26. 8g, Dietary Fiber 1. 9g, Total Sugars 5. 6g, Protein 11. 9g

Tasty Mac and Cheese

Preparation Time: 05 minutes
Cooking Time: 10 minutes
Servings: 2
Ingredients:
- ½ cup of soy milk
- 1 cup dry macaroni
- Enough water
- ½ cup shredded mozzarella cheese
- ¼ teaspoon salt
- ¼ teaspoon Dijon mustard
- 1/8 teaspoon red chili powder

Directions:
1. Add macaroni, soy milk, water, and salt, chili powder, Dijon mustard to the Instant Pot.
2. Place lid on Instant Pot and lock into place to seal.
3. Pressure Cook on High Pressure for 4 minutes.
4. Use Quick Pressure Release.
5. Stir cheese into macaroni and then stir in the cheeses until melted and combined.

Nutrition: Calories 210, Total Fat 3g, Saturated Fat 1g, Cholesterol 4mg, Sodium 374mg, Total Carbohydrate 35. 7g, Dietary Fiber 1. 8g, Total Sugars 3. 6g, Protein 9. 6g

Jackfruit and Red Pepper Pasta

Preparation Time: 05 minutes
Cooking Time: 17 minutes
Servings: 2
Ingredients:
- ½ cup gnocchi
- 1/8 cup avocado oil

- ½ tablespoon garlic powder
- 1/2 teaspoon crushed red pepper
- ½ bunch fresh mint
- ½ cup jackfruit
- Salt to taste
- Enough water

Directions:
1. Set Instant Pot to Sauté.
2. Add the avocado oil and allow it to sizzle.
3. Add the garlic powder and cook for 2 minutes.
4. Stir regularly.
5. Add jackfruit and cook until about 4 - 5 minutes.
6. Add gnocchi, water, fresh mint, salt, and red pepper into Instant Pot.
7. Lock the lid and make sure the vent is closed.
8. Set Instant Pot to Manual or Pressure Cook on High PRESSURE for 10 minutes.
9. When cooking time ends, release pressure and wait for steam to completely stop before opening the lid.
10.   Enjoy.

Nutrition: Calories 110, Total Fat 2. 3g, Saturated Fat 0. 4g, Cholesterol 0mg, Sodium 168mg, Total Carbohydrate 21. 5g, Dietary Fiber 2. 5g, Total Sugars 0. 6g, Protein 2. 3g

Creamy Mushroom Pasta with Broccoli

Preparation Time: 05 minutes
Cooking Time: 12 minutes
Servings: 2
Ingredients:
- 1 tablespoon coconut oil
- 1 small onion
- ½ teaspoon garlic powder
- 1 cup mushrooms
- 1 tablespoon coconut flour
- 1 cup of water
- ¼ cup red wine
- 1/8 cup coconut cream
- ¼ teaspoon dried basil
- Salt and pepper to taste
- 1/8 bunch fresh cilantro
- ½ cup mozzarella cheese
- 4 oz. pasta
- ½ cup broccoli

Directions:
1. Set Instant Pot to Sauté.

2. Add the coconut oil and allow it to sizzle.
3. Add coconut flour and mushrooms, sauté for 2 minutes.
4. Stir regularly.
5. It will coat the mushrooms and will begin to turn golden in color.
6. Just make sure to keep stirring so that the flour does not burn.
7. Combine water along with the red wine, basil, salt, and pepper.
8. Whisk until no flour lumps remain.
9. Add pasta, broccoli, cilantro, onion, and garlic powder.
10. Lock the lid and make sure the vent is closed.
11. Set Instant Pot to Manual or Pressure Cook on High Pressure for 10 minutes.
12. When cooking time ends, release pressure and wait for steam to completely stop before opening the lid.
13. Stir in cheese and coconut cream.
14. Serve hot and enjoy.

Nutrition: Calories 363, Total Fat 14. 2g, Saturated Fat 11g, Cholesterol 45mg, Sodium 91mg, Total Carbohydrate 43. 4g, Dietary Fiber 4. 6g, Total Sugars 3. 9g, Protein 12. 1g

Peanut Noodles Stir Fry

Preparation Time: 05 minutes
Cooking Time: 17 minutes
Servings: 2
Ingredients:
- ½ teaspoon ginger powder
- ¼ cup natural peanut butter
- ¼ cup hoisin sauce
- 1 cup hot water
- ¼ teaspoon sriracha hot sauce
- 1 tablespoon vegetable oil
- ½ teaspoon garlic powder
- 1 cup frozen stir fry vegetables
- 2 oz. soba noodles
- 2 sliced leek, optional

Directions:
1. Prepare the sauce first.

2. Add ginger powder into a bowl.
3. Add the peanut butter, hoisin sauce, sriracha hot sauce, and ¼ cup of hot water.
4. Stir or whisk until smooth.
5. Set the sauce aside until it is needed.
6. Set the Instant Pot to Sauté.
7. Add the vegetable oil and allow it to sizzle.
8. Add garlic powder and ginger powder and cook for 2 minutes.
9. Add the bag of frozen vegetables and cook for 5 minutes.
10. Add the remaining water and soba noodles.
11. Lock the lid and make sure the vent is closed.
12. Set Instant Pot to Manual or Pressure Cook on High Pressure for 10 minutes.
13. When cooking time ends, release pressure and wait for steam to completely stop before opening the lid.
14. Stir until everything is combined and coated with sauce.
15. Garnish with sliced leek if desired.

Nutrition: Calories 501, Total Fat 24. 4g, Saturated Fat 4. 6g, Cholesterol 1mg, Sodium 788mg, Total Carbohydrate 58. 1g, Dietary Fiber 6g, Total Sugars 15. 8g, Protein 17. 3g

Cauliflower Shells Cheese

Preparation Time: 05 minutes
Cooking Time: 15 minutes
Servings: 2
Ingredients:
• 4 oz. macaroni
• 1 cup vegetable broth
• ½ cup cauliflower florets
• 1/2 small onion
• 1 1/2 tablespoons butter
• 1 1/2 tablespoons coconut flour
• 1 1/2 cups coconut milk
• 1 cup sharp cheddar, shredded
• Salt and pepper to taste
Directions:
Set the Instant Pot to Sauté, add the coconut flour, butter, and onion.
The flour and butter will form a paste, whisk for 1-2 minutes more taking care not to let it scorch.

This slightly cooks the flour preventing the cheese sauce from having an overly strong flour flavor or paste-like flavor.
• Whisk the milk into the roux until no lumps remain.
Add some freshly cracked pepper to the sauce.
Bring the mixture up to a simmer, stirring often.
Set aside.
Add macaroni and vegetable broth into Instant Pot.
Lock the lid and make sure the vent is closed.
Add cauliflower and set Instant Pot to Manual or Pressure Cook on High Pressure for 10 minutes.
When cooking time ends, release pressure and wait for steam to completely stop before opening the lid.
Add cheddar and stir sauce mix well with macaroni.

Nutrition: Calories 643, Total Fat 53. 6g, Saturated Fat 42. 1g, Cholesterol 75mg, Sodium 443mg, Total Carbohydrate 26. 2g, Dietary Fiber 6. 6g, Total Sugars 6. 2g, Protein 18. 4g

Chickpea Sunflower Sandwich

Preparation Time: 15 minutes

Cooking Time: 10 minutes

Servings: 2

Ingredients:

For The Sandwich:

- 1 ¾ cup cooked chickpeas
- 1/4 cup chopped red onion
- 1/4 cup roasted sunflower seeds, unsalted
- ½ teaspoon salt
- ¼ teaspoon ground black pepper
- 1 tablespoon maple syrup
- 1/2 teaspoon Dijon mustard
- 3 tablespoons vegan mayonnaise
- 2 tablespoons fresh dill
- 4 pieces of rustic bread

For The Garlic Herb Sauce:

- 1 teaspoon minced garlic
- 1/2 of lemon, juiced

- ½ teaspoon of sea salt
- 1 teaspoon dried dill
- ¼ dried dill
- 1/4 cup hummus
- ¼ cup almond milk, unsweetened

For Topping:
- 1 avocado, pitted, sliced
- 1 medium white onion, peeled, sliced
- ½ cup chopped lettuce
- 1 medium tomato, sliced

Directions:
1. Prepare the garlic herb sauce and for this, take a medium bowl, place all of its ingredients and whisk until combined, set aside until combined.
2. Take a medium bowl, add chickpeas in it, and then mash by using a fork until broken.
3. Then add onion, dill, sunflower seeds, salt, black pepper, mustard, maple syrup, and mayonnaise and stir until well combined.
4. Take a medium skillet pan, place it over medium heat, add bread slices, and cook for 3 minutes per side until toasted.
5. Spread chickpea mixture on one side of two bread slices, top with prepared garlic herb sauce, avocado, onion, tomato, and lettuce and cover with the other two slices.
6. Serve straight away.

Nutrition: 532 Cal 30 g Fat 4 g Saturated Fat 52 g Carbohydrates 14 g Fiber 8 g Sugars 17 g Protein;

White Bean and Artichoke Sandwich

Preparation Time: 15 minutes

Cooking Time: 10 minutes

Servings: 4

Ingredients:

- 1 ¼ cooked white beans
- ½ cup cashew nuts
- 6 artichoke hearts, chopped
- ¼ cup sunflower seeds, hulled
- 1 clove of garlic, peeled
- ¼ teaspoon salt
- ¼ teaspoon ground black pepper
- 1 teaspoon dried rosemary
- 1 lemon, grated
- 6 tablespoons almond milk, unsweetened
- 8 pieces of rustic bread

Directions:

1. Soak cashew nuts in warm water for 10 minutes, then drain them and transfer into a food processor.
2. Add garlic, salt, black pepper, rosemary, lemon zest, and milk and then pulse for 2 minutes until smooth, scraping the sides of the container frequently.
3. Take a medium bowl, place beans in it, mash them by using a fork, then add sunflower seeds and artichokes and stir until mixed.
4. Pour in cashew nuts dressing, stir until coated, and taste to adjust seasoning.
5. Take a medium skillet pan, place it over medium heat, add bread slices, and cook for 3 minutes per side until toasted.
6. Spread white beans mixture on one side of four bread slices and then cover with the other four slices.
7. Serve straight away.

Nutrition: 220 Cal 8 g Fat 1 g Saturated Fat 28 g Carbohydrates 8 g Fiber 2 g Sugars 12 g Protein;

Sabich Sandwich

Preparation Time: 10 minutes
Cooking Time: 10 minutes
Servings: 4
Ingredients:

- 1/2 cup cooked white beans
- 2 medium potatoes, peeled, boiled,
- ½-inch thick sliced
- 1 medium eggplant, destemmed,
- ½-inch cubed
- 4 dill pickles,
- ¼-inch thick sliced
- ¼ teaspoon of sea salt
- 2 tablespoons olive oil
- 1/4 teaspoon harissa paste
- 1/2 cup hummus
- 1 tablespoon mayonnaise
- 4 pita bread pockets
- 1/2 cup tabbouleh salad

Directions:

1. Take a small frying pan, place it over medium-low heat, add oil and wait until it gets hot.
2. Season eggplant pieces with salt, add to the hot frying pan and cook for 8 minutes until softened, and when done, remove the pan from heat.
3. Take a small bowl, place white beans in it, add harissa paste and mayonnaise and then stir until combined.
4. Assemble the sandwich and for this, place pita bread on clean working space, smear generously with hummus, then cover half of each pita bread with potato slices and top with a dill pickle slices.

5. Spoon 2 tablespoons of white bean mixture on each dill pickle, top with 3 tablespoons of cooked eggplant pieces and 2 tablespoons of tabbouleh salad and then cover the filling with the other half of pita bread.

6. Serve straight away.

Nutrition: 386 Cal 13 g Fat 2 g Saturated Fat 56 g Carbohydrates 7 g Fiber 3 g Sugars 12 g Protein;

Tofu and Pesto Sandwich

Preparation Time: 10 minutes
Cooking Time: 15 minutes
Servings: 4
Ingredients:

- 2 blocks of tofu, firm, pressed, drain
- 8 slices of tomato
- 8 leaves of lettuce
- 1 ½ teaspoon dried oregano
- ½ cup green pesto
- 2 tablespoons olive oil
- 8 slices of sandwich bread

Directions:

1. Switch on the oven, then set it to 375 degrees F and let it preheat.

2. Cut tofu into thick slices, place them in a baking sheet, drizzle with oil and sprinkle with oregano, and bake the tofu pieces for 15 minutes until roasted.

3. Assemble the sandwich and for this, spread pesto on one side of each bread slice, then top four slices with lettuce, tomato slices, and roasted tofu and then cover with the other four slices.

4. Serve straight away.

Nutrition: 277 Cal 9.1 g Fat 1.5 g Saturated Fat 33.1 g Carbohydrates 3.6 g Fiber 12.7 g Sugars 16.1 g Protein;

Chickpea and Mayonnaise Salad Sandwich

Preparation Time: 10 minutes
Cooking Time: 0 minutes
Servings: 4
Ingredients:
For the mayonnaise:

- 1/3 cup cashew nuts, soaked in boiling water for 10 minutes
- ½ teaspoon ground black pepper
- 1 teaspoon salt
- 6 teaspoons apple cider vinegar
- 2 teaspoon maple syrup
- 1/2 teaspoon Dijon mustard

For the chickpea salad:

- 1 small bunch of chives, chopped
- 1 ½ cup sweetcorn
- 3 cups cooked chickpeas

To serve:

- 4 sandwich bread
- 4 leaves of lettuce
- ½ cup chopped cherry tomatoes

Directions:

1. Prepare the mayonnaise and for this, place all of its ingredients in a food processor and then pulse for 2 minutes until smooth, scraping the sides of the container frequently.
2. Take a medium bowl, place chickpeas in it, and then mash by using a fork until broken.

3. Add chives and corn, stir until mixed, then add mayonnaise and stir until well combined.

4. Assemble the sandwich and for this, stuff sandwich bread with chickpea salad, top each sandwich with a lettuce leaf, and ¼ cup of chopped tomatoes and then serve.

Nutrition: 387 Cal 19 g Fat 5 g Saturated Fat 39.7 g Carbohydrates 7.2 g Fiber 4.6 g Sugars 10 g Protein;

Tropical Island Burgers

Preparation time: 10 minutes
Cooking time: 30 minutes
Servings: 6–8 burgers
Ingredients:

- 3 cups canned black beans, rinsed and drained
- 1/2 cup rolled oats
- 4 tablespoons sweet corn
- 1/4 cup crushed pineapple
- 1 teaspoon mustard
- Salt, pepper (to taste)

Directions:

1. Create a paste with beans and oats by pulsing in food processor.

2. In a large mixing bowl, combine paste with remaining ingredient list.

3. Using wet hands, form the mixture into a burger shape.

4. Add one tablespoon of olive oil to frying pan and heat over medium.

5. Cook burgers on each side 7 minutes, until brown and crispy.

Nutrition: 230 Cal 5.8 g Fat 1.7 g Saturated Fat 34.3 g Carbohydrates 1.5 g Fiber

Fennel and Beetroot Burger

Preparation time: 10 minutes

Cooking time: 50 minutes

Servings: 6–8 burgers

Ingredients:

- 2 medium size beetroots, peeled and grated
- 2 tablespoons chopped dill
- 1 fennel bulb, trimmed and finely chopped
- 1 cup cooked brown rice
- 2 tablespoons cornmeal
- 1/4 cup tomato sauce
- Salt, pepper (tp taste)

Directions:

1. In a large mixing bowl, combine grated beets, fennel, dill, brown rice and cornmeal.

2. Stir in the tomato sauce, salt/pepper, form small patties.

3. Add one tablespoon of olive oil to frying pan and fry burger for 6 minutes on each side.

4. Serve on vegan burger buns and favorite toppings

Nutrition: 218.5 Cal 5.2 g Fat 1.5 g Saturated Fat 32.3 g Carbohydrates 1.3 g Fiber

Sautéed Green Beans, Mushrooms & Tomatoes

Preparation Time: 15 minutes

Cooking Time: 15 minutes

Servings: 10

Ingredients:

- Water 3 lb. green beans, trimmed
- 2 tablespoons olive oil
- 8 cloves garlic, minced
- ½ cup tomato, diced
- 12 oz. cremini mushrooms, sliced into quarters
- Salt and pepper to taste

Directions:

1. Fill a pot with water.
2. Bring to a boil.
3. Add the beans and cook for 5 minutes.
4. Drain the beans.
5. Dry the pot.
6. Pour oil into the pot.
7. Add garlic, tomato and mushrooms.
8. Cook for 5 minutes.
9. Add the beans and cook for another 5 minutes.
10. Season with salt and pepper.
11. Store in a food container and reheat before eating.

Nutrition: 230.5 Cal 5.6 g Fat 1.8 g Saturated Fat 32.3 g Carbohydrates 1.3 g Fiber

Green Beans, Roasted Red Peppers & Onions

Preparation Time: 15 minutes
Cooking Time: 25 minutes
Servings: 6
Ingredients:

- 1 tablespoon olive oil
- 1 ½ cups onion, chopped
- 1 tablespoon red wine vinegar
- ½ cup jarred roasted red peppers, drained and chopped
- 2 tablespoons fresh basil, chopped
- ¼ cup olives, pitted and sliced
- Salt and pepper to taste

- 1 lb. fresh green beans, trimmed and sliced

Directions:

1. Pour olive oil in a pan over medium heat.
2. Add onion and cook for 10 minutes.
3. Pour in the vinegar.
4. Cook for 2 minutes.
5. Add roasted red peppers, basil and olives.
6. Season with salt and pepper.
7. Remove from the stove.
8. In a saucepan with water, cook beans for 10 minutes.
9. Add beans to the onion mixture.
10. Stir for 3 minutes.

Nutrition: 208.5 Cal 5.2 g Fat 1.6 g Saturated Fat 29.3 g Carbohydrates 1.3 g Fiber

Sweet Spicy Beans

Preparation Time: 10 minutes
Cooking Time: 50 minutes
Servings: 10
Ingredients:

1. 3 tablespoons vegetable oil
2. 1 onion, chopped
3. 45 oz. navy beans, rinsed and drained
4. 1 ½ cups water
5. ¾ cup ketchup
6. ⅓ cup brown sugar
7. 1 tablespoon white vinegar
8. 1 teaspoon chipotle peppers in adobo sauce
9. Salt and pepper to taste

Directions:

1. Pour the oil in a pan over medium heat.
2. Add onion and cook for 10 minutes.

3. Add the rest of the Ingredients.
4. Bring to a boil.
5. Reduce heat and simmer for 30 minutes.
6. Transfer to food container.
7. Reheat when ready to eat.

Nutrition: 228.5 Cal 5.5 g Fat 1.7 g Saturated Fat 32.3 g Carbohydrates 1.3 g Fiber

Barbecue Sauce

Preparation time: 5 minutes
Cooking time: 0 minute
Servings: 16
Ingredients:

- 8 ounces tomato sauce
- 1 teaspoon garlic powder
- ¼ teaspoon ground black pepper
- 1/2 teaspoon. sea salt
- 2 Tablespoons Dijon mustard
- 3 packets stevia
- 1 teaspoon molasses
- 1 Tablespoon apple cider vinegar
- 2 Tablespoons tamari
- 1 teaspoon liquid aminos

Directions:

1. Take a medium bowl, place all the ingredients in it, and stir until combined. Serve straight away

Nutrition: Calories 110, Cholesterol 0mg, Sodium 168mg, Total Carbohydrate 21. 5g, Dietary Fiber 2. 5g, Total Sugars 0. 6g, Protein 2. 3g

Bolognese Sauce

Preparation time: 10 minutes
Cooking time: 45 minutes
Servings: 8
Ingredients:

- ½ of small green bell pepper, chopped
- 1 stalk of celery, chopped
- 1 small carrot, chopped
- 1 medium white onion, peeled, chopped
- 2 teaspoons minced garlic
- 1/2 teaspoon crushed red pepper flakes
- 3 tablespoons olive oil
- 8-ounce tempeh, crumbled
- 8 ounces white mushrooms, chopped
- 1/2 cup dried red lentils
- 28-ounce crushed tomatoes
- 28-ounce whole tomatoes, chopped
- 1 teaspoon dried oregano
- 1/2 teaspoon fennel seed
- 1/2 teaspoon ground black pepper
- 1/2 teaspoon salt
- 1 teaspoon dried basil
- 1/4 cup chopped parsley
- 1 bay leaf
- 6-ounce tomato paste
- 1 cup dry red wine

Directions:

2. Take a Dutch oven, place it over medium heat, add oil, and when hot, add the first six ingredients, stir and cook for 5 minutes until sauté.
3. Then switch heat to medium-high level, add two ingredients after olive oil, stir and cook for 3 minutes.
4. Switch heat to medium-low level, stir in tomato paste, and continue cooking for 2 minutes.

5. Add remaining ingredients except for lentils, stir and bring the mixture to boil.
6. Switch heat to the low level, simmer sauce for 10 minutes, covering the pan partially, then add lentils and continue cooking for 20 minutes until tender.
7. Serve sauce with cooked

Nutrition: Calories 100, Total Fat 2. 3g, Saturated Fat 0. 7g, Cholesterol 0mg, Sodium 168mg, Total Carbohydrate 21. 5g, Protein 2. 3g

Marsala Carrots

Preparation Time: 5 Minutes
Cooking Time: 20 Minutes
Serves: 4
Ingredients:

- 2 tablespoons vegan margarine
- 1 pound carrots, cut diagonally into
- ¼-inch slices
- Salt and freshly ground black pepper
- ½ cup Marsala
- ¼ cup water
- ¼ cup chopped fresh parsley, for garnish

Direction:

1. In a large skillet, melt the margarine over medium heat.
2. Add the carrots and mix well to coat evenly with the margarine.
3. Cover and cook, stirring occasionally, for 5 minutes.
4. Season with salt and pepper to taste, stirring to coat.
5. Add the Marsala and the water.

6. Reduce heat to low, cover and simmer until carrots are tender, about 15 minutes.
7. Uncover and cook over medium-high heat until the liquid has reduced to a syrupy sauce, stirring to prevent burning.
8. Transfer to a serving bowl and sprinkle with parsley.
9. Serve immediately.

Nutrition: Calories: 313 Cal Fat: 14 g Carbs: 47.8 g Protein: 8.2 g Fiber: 11.4 g

Spaghetti with Mushrooms

Preparation Time: 10 minutes
Cooking time: 60 minutes
Servings: 4
Ingredients:

- 2 pounds spaghetti squash, halved
- 1 tablespoon unsalted butter
- 2 tablespoons olive oil
- ½ of a white onion, peeled, chopped
- 16 ounces sliced cremini mushrooms
- 2 teaspoons minced garlic
- 3 tablespoons sage
- 2/3 teaspoon salt
- 1/3 teaspoon ground black pepper
- 1/8 teaspoon nutmeg
- ¼ cup grated vegan parmesan cheese

Direction:

1. Bake squash on a parchment-lined baking sheet or 50 minutes at 400 degrees F until tender.
2. Meanwhile, take a large skillet pan, place it medium-high heat, add oil and butter and when hot, add onion and

cook for 3 minutes until tender.

3. Then add mushrooms, switch heat to medium level, and cook for 7 minutes.

4. Stir in sage and garlic, cook for 4 minutes until mushrooms have turned brown, and then season with black pepper, nutmeg and salt.

5. When squash has roasted, pierce it with a fork, let it cool for 10 minutes, then remove its seeds and scoop the flesh of the squash to a saucepan.

6. Add mushrooms, stir until mixed, season with some more salt, and stir in cheese until incorporated.

7. Serve straight away.

Nutrition: Calories: 313 Cal Fat: 14 g Carbs: 47.8 g Protein: 8.2 g Fiber: 11.4 g

Avocado Linguine

Preparation Time: 10 minutes
Cooking time: 0 minute
Servings: 4
Ingredients:
- ½ cup arugula
- 2 medium avocados
- 2 cloves of garlic, peeled
- 1/4 teaspoon ground white pepper
- 3/4 teaspoons salt
- 1 teaspoon lemon zest
- 3 tablespoons lemon juice
- 3 tablespoons olive oil
- 8 ounces linguine, whole-wheat, boiled

Direction:
1. Prepare the avocado sauce, and for this, place all the Shopping List: in a food

processor, except for pasta, arugula, pepper, and lemon zest and pulse until smooth.

2. Tip the puree in a large bowl, add remaining Shopping List:, toss until well mixed and taste to adjust seasoning.

3. Serve straight away.

Nutrition: Calories: 387 Cal Fat: 16.6 g Carbs: 54.3 g Protein: 9.4 g Fiber: 8.6 g

Baked Beans

Preparation Time: 5 Minutes
Cooking Time: 45 Minutes
Serves: 4
Ingredients:

- 1 tablespoon extra-virgin olive oil
- 1 medium yellow onion, minced
- 3 garlic cloves, minced
- 1 (14.5-ounce) can crushed tomatoes
- ½ cup pure maple syrup
- 2 tablespoons blackstrap molasses
- 1 tablespoon soy sauce
- 1½ teaspoons dry mustard
- ¼ teaspoon ground cayenne
- Salt and freshly ground black pepper
- 3 cups cooked or 2 (15.5-ounce) cans Great Northern beans, drained and rinsed

Direction:

1. Preheat the oven to 350 ° F.
2. Lightly grease a 2-quart saucepan and set aside.
3. In a large saucepan, heat the oil over medium heat.
4. Add the onion and garlic.
5. Cover and cook until softened for about 5 minutes.
6. Stir in the tomatoes, maple syrup, molasses, soy sauce,

mustard, and cayenne pepper and bring to a boil.

7. Reduce the heat to low and simmer, uncovered, until slightly reduced for about 10 minutes.
8. Season with salt and pepper.
9. Put the beans in the prepared saucepan.
10.   Add the sauce, stirring to mix and coat the beans.
11. Cover and cook until hot and bubbly for about 30 minutes.
12. Serve immediately

Nutrition: Calories: 250 Cal Fat: 14 g Carbs: 29 g Protein: 8 g Fiber: 12 g

Lemony Quinoa

Preparation Time: 10 minutes
Cooking time: 0 minute
Servings: 6

Ingredients:
- 1 cup quinoa, cooked
- 1/4 of medium red onion, peeled, chopped
- 1 bunch of parsley, chopped
- 2 stalks of celery, chopped
- ¼ teaspoon of sea salt
- 1/4 teaspoon cayenne pepper
- 1/2 teaspoon ground cumin
- 1/4 cup lemon juice
- 1/4 cup pine nuts, toasted

Direction:
1. Take a large bowl, place all the Shopping List: in it, and stir until combined.
2. Serve straight away.

Nutrition: Calories: 147 Cal Fat: 4.8 g Carbs: 21.4 g Protein: 6 g Fiber: 3 g

Vegan Curried Rice

Preparation Time: 5 minutes
Cooking time: 25 minutes
Servings: 4
Ingredients:

- 1 cup white rice
- 1 tablespoon minced garlic
- 1 tablespoon ground curry powder
- 1/3 teaspoon ground black pepper
- 1 tablespoon red chili powder
- 1 tablespoon ground cumin
- 2 tablespoons olive oil
- 1 tablespoon soy sauce
- 1 cup vegetable broth

Direction:

1. Take a saucepan, put it on low heat, add the oil and when it is hot add the garlic and cook for 3 minutes.
2. Then add all the spices, cook for 1 minute until fragrant, pour in the broth and bring the heat to a high level.
3. Stir in the soy sauce, bring the mixture to a boil, add the rice, stir until combined, then turn the heat to low and simmer for 20 minutes until the rice is tender and all the liquid is absorbed.
4. Serve immediately.

Nutrition: Calories: 262 Cal Fat: 8 g Carbs: 43 g Protein: 5 g Fiber: 2 g

Red Bean

Preparation Time: 5 Minutes
Cooking Time: 45 Minutes
Serves: 4
Ingredients:

- 1 tablespoon extra-virgin olive oil
- 1 medium yellow onion chopped
- 2 celery ribs chopped
- 1 medium green bell pepper, chopped
- 3 garlic cloves, minced
- 1 cup long-grain rice
- 3 cups cooked or 2 (15.5-ounce) cans dark red kidney beans, drained and rinsed
- 1 (14.5-ounce) can diced tomatoes, drained
- 1 (14.5-ounce) can crushed tomatoes
- 1 (4-ounce) can mild green chiles drained
- 1 teaspoon dried thyme
- ½ teaspoon dried marjoram
- 1 teaspoon salt Freshly ground black pepper
- 2½cups vegetable broth, or water
- 1 tablespoon chopped fresh parsley, for garnish
- Tabasco sauce (optional)

Direction:

1. In a large saucepan, heat the oil over medium heat.
2. Add the onion, celery, pepper and garlic.
3. Cover and cook until softened for about 7 minutes.
4. Stir in the rice, beans, diced tomatoes, crushed tomatoes, chillies, thyme, marjoram, salt and black pepper.
5. Add broth, cover, then simmer until vegetables are soft and rice is tender, about 45 minutes.
6. Sprinkle with parsley and a splash of Tabasco if using and serve.

Nutrition: Calories: 262 Cal Fat: 8 g Carbs: 43 g Protein: 5 g Fiber: 2 g

Chili

Preparation Time: 5 Minutes
Cooking Time: 55 Minutes
Serves: 4
Ingredients:

- 1 small butternut squash, peeled, halved, and seeded
- 1 tablespoon extra-virgin olive oil
- 1 medium onion, chopped
- 3 cups mild tomato salsa, homemade or store-bought
- 3 cups cooked or 2 (15.5-ounce) cans pinto beans, drained and rinsed
- 1 cup frozen lima beans
- 1 cup fresh or frozen corn kernels
- 1 canned chipotle chile in adobo, minced
- 1 cup water
- 3 tablespoons chili powder
- ½ teaspoon ground allspice
- ½ teaspoon sugar
- Salt and freshly ground black pepper

Direction:

1. Cut the squash into ¼-inch cubes and set aside.
2. In a large saucepan, heat the oil over medium heat.
3. Add the onion and squash, cover and cook until softened for about 10 minutes.
4. Add the salsa, pinto beans, lima beans, corn and chipotle pepper.
5. Mix the chili powder, allspice, sugar, salt and black pepper in the water.
6. Bring to a boil, then reduce the heat to medium and simmer, covered, until the vegetables are tender for about 45 minutes.
7. Uncover and simmer for about 10 minutes more.
8. Serve immediately.

Nutrition: Calories: 252 Cal Fat: 9 g Carbs: 43 g Protein: 5 g Fiber: 2 g

Butternut Squash, Onion, and Tomato Fry

Preparation Time: 40 minutes
Cooking Time: 15/20 minutes
Servings: 2
Ingredients:

- Butternut squash: 2 cups
- Ripe tomatoes: 2 chopped
- Onion: 1 roughly chopped
- Garlic: 2 cloves roughly chopped
- Ginger: 1 tbsp peeled and chopped
- Ground turmeric:1 tsp
- Cinnamon stick: 1/2
- Cumin seeds: 2 tsp
- Green chilies: 2 chopped
- Ground red chili: ½ tsp
- Coriander: ½ cup chopped
- Olive oil: 2 tbsp

Direction:

1. In a large pan, add two tablespoons of oil
2. Add in onion, ginger, and garlic and stir and cook for 5 minutes
3. Add tomatoes and cover and cook for 5 minutes
4. Add all the spices, combine and leave for 2 minutes
5. Add butternut squash and stir for 5 minutes
6. Then cover and cook till oil appears on the surface
7. When done top with green chilies and coriander serve with rice

Nutrition: Amount Per Serving Carbs:41.45g Protein: 3.5g Fats: 28.6g Calories: 158Kcal

Burrito Vegan Bowl

Preparation Time: 2 hours 30 minutes

Cooking Time: 0 minutes

Servings: 2

Ingredients:

- Sweetcorn: 100g drained
- Pinto beans: 200g tin rinsed and drained
- Avocado: ½ small
- Roasted red peppers: 2 from a jar chopped
- Red onion: ½ small finely chopped
- Lime: 1 plus wedges to serve
- Red chili: 1 seeded and diced
- Cashew nuts: 100g
- Baby spinach: 100g shredded
- Young kale: 75g stalks discarded and shredded
- Olive oil
- Chipotle paste 1 tsp

Direction:

1. Put cashew nuts in cold water in a bowl and cover it with plastic wrap and leave for 2 hours or overnight
2. Now drain the water out and put the cashew in a blender
3. Add 100 ml of water to the blender and blend it till it becomes smooth
4. Now slowly add more and more water to the get a double cream
5. Take 4 tablespoons of cashew cream and mix it with chipotle paste
6. Now add 1 teaspoon lime juice and add seasoning
7. You can keep the remaining cream in a container and cover it and let it rest in the chill
8. The cream will last for 3-4 days but it will need to be stirred back

9. Put the chili, pinto beans, red onion and sweetcorn with 1 teaspoon of lime juice and add seasoning
10. Now pound the avocado with remaining onion and chili and put the remaining lemon juice
11. Now put in the spinach and kale with ½ teaspoon oil until all leaves get coated with oil
12. Now place the mixture in two deep bowls and add sweetcorn salsa on top with mashed avocados and diced red peppers
13. Now pour over the dressing and serve

Nutrition: Amount Per Serving Carbs: 30.4g Protein: 13.5g Fats: 14.9g Calories: 324Kcal

Cauli Patty

Preparation Time: 45 minutes
Cooking Time: 30 minutes
Servings: 2
Ingredients:
- Olive oil: 2 tbsp
- Cauliflower: 2 cups cut in big florets
- Rice vinegar: 1 tbsp
- Onion: 1 finely diced
- Salt: as per your taste
- Pepper: as per your taste
- Coriander: ¼ cup finely chopped

Direction:
1. Preheat the oven 200C
2. Add cauliflowers to the baking sheet and sprinkle seasoning and brush with olive oil
3. Roast for 25 minutes till they turn golden and soft
4. Remove from oven mash using a potato masher

5. Add to the bowl and mix salt, coriander, onion, and pepper
6. Make round balls from it and press to form patties
7. Add oil to the non-stick pan and fry from both sides for 3-4 minutes

Nutrition: Amount Per Serving Carbs: 43.75g Protein:6.4g Fats: 13.3g Calories: 164.75Kcal

Cauli Rice with Fajita Bowl

Preparation Time: 30 minutes
Cooking Time: 45 minutes
Servings: 2
Ingredients:
- Cauliflower: 1 chopped
- Chopped tomatoes: 200g tin
- Red peppers: 2 sliced
- Avocado: ½ small sliced
- Olive oil
- Dried oregano: ½ tsp
- Chipotle paste: 1 tbsp
- Chili flakes: ½ tsp
- Red onion: 1 sliced
- Smoked paprika: ½ tsp
- Cumin seeds: ½ tsp
- Garlic salt: ½ tsp
- Salt: as per your need
- Pepper: as per your need
- Coriander: 2 tbsp chopped
- Lime wedges to serve

Direction:
1. Take a pan and heat one tablespoon oil
2. Add onions and peppers and fry for 20 minutes
3. Add tomatoes, smoked paprika, and chipotle paste and stir and add some water
4. Cook for 20 minutes to thicken the sauce
5. Add cauliflower to the food processor and grind it till it appears like a grain

6. Take a frying pan and add a tablespoon of olive oil and heat
7. Add cumin, garlic salt, chili flakes, and oregano and fry for a minute
8. Then include cauliflower rice and stir
9. Cook for 5 minutes and season with pepper
10. Spread cauli rice on the plate and top with the sauce, avocado, and coriander leaves
11. Serve with lime wedges

Nutrition: Amount Per Serving Carbs: 22.1 g Protein: 7 g Fats: 4.4 g Calories: 174 Kcal

Chana Chat

Preparation Time: 10 minutes
Cooking Time: 0 minutes

Servings: 2
Ingredients:

- Chickpeas: 2 cups rinsed and drained
- Chaat masala: 2 tsp
- Lime: 1 juiced
- Onion: 1 diced
- Tomato: 1 diced
- Sea salt: ½ tsp
- Coriander: ½ cup
- Mint: ¼ cup
- Vegan yogurt: ½ cup

Direction:

1. Place all the ingredients in a large bowl
2. Combine them well and serve

Nutrition: Amount Per Serving Carbs: 65g Protein: 18g Fats: 5.5g Calories: 380Kcal

Stir Fry Noodles

Preparation Time: 10 minutes
Cooking Time: 8 minutes
Servings: 4
Ingredients:

- 1 cup broccoli, chopped
- 1 cup red bell pepper, chopped
- 1 cup mushrooms, chopped
- 1 large onion, chopped
- 1 batch Stir Fry Sauce, prepared
- Salt and black pepper, to taste
- 2 cups spaghetti, cooked
- 4 garlic cloves, minced
- 2 tablespoons sesame oil

Directions:

1. Heat sesame oil in a pan over medium heat and add garlic, onions, bell pepper, broccoli, mushrooms.
2. Sauté for about 5 minutes and add spaghetti noodles and stir fry sauce.
3. Mix well and cook for 3 more minutes.
4. Dish out in plates and serve to enjoy.

Nutrition: Calories: 567 Fat: 48g Carbs: 6g Fiber: 4g Protein: 33g

Spicy Sweet Chili Veggie Noodles

Preparation Time: 10 minutes
Cooking Time: 7 minutes
Servings: 2
Ingredients:

- 1 head of broccoli, cut into bite sized florets
- 1 onion, finely sliced
- 1 tablespoon olive oil
- 1 courgette, halved

- 2 nests of whole-wheat noodles
- 5 oz. mushrooms, sliced

For Sauce:
- 3 tablespoons soy sauce
- ¼ cup sweet chili sauce
- 1 teaspoon Sriracha
- 1 tablespoon peanut butter
- 2 tablespoons boiled water

For Topping:
- 2 teaspoons sesame seeds
- 2 teaspoons dried chili flakes

Directions:
1. Heat olive oil on medium heat in a saucepan and add onions.
2. Sauté for about 2 minutes and add broccoli, courgette and mushrooms.
3. Cook for about 5 minutes, stirring occasionally.
4. Whisk sweet chili sauce, soy sauce, Sriracha, water and peanut butter in a bowl.
5. Cook the noodles according to packet instructions and add to the vegetables.
6. Stir in the sauce and top with dried chili flakes and sesame seeds to serve.

Nutrition: Calories: 351 Fat: 27g Protein: 25g Carbs: 2g Fiber: 1g

Creamy Vegan Mushroom Pasta

Preparation Time: 10 minutes
Cooking Time: 30 minutes
Servings: 6
Ingredients:
- 2 cups frozen peas, thawed
- 3 tablespoons flour, unbleached
- 3 cups almond breeze, unsweetened
- 1 tablespoon nutritional yeast

- 1/3 cup fresh parsley, chopped, plus extra for garnish
- ¼ cup olive oil
- 1-pound pasta of choice
- 4 cloves garlic, minced
- 2/3 cup shallots, chopped
- 8 cups mixed mushrooms, sliced
- Salt and black pepper, to taste

Directions:

1. Take a bowl and boil pasta in salted water.
2. Heat olive oil in a pan over medium heat.
3. Add mushrooms, garlic, shallots and ½ tsp salt and cook for 15 minutes.
4. Sprinkle flour on the vegetables and stir for a minute while cooking.
5. Add almond beverage, stir constantly.
6. Let it simmer for 5 minutes and add pepper to it.
7. Cook for 3 more minutes and remove from heat. Stir in nutritional yeast.
8. Add peas, salt, and pepper.
9. Cook for another minute and add
10. Add pasta to this sauce.
11. Garnish and serve!

Nutrition: Calories: 364 Fat: 28g Protein: 24g Carbs: 24g Fiber: 2g 150.

Vegan Chinese Noodles

Preparation Time: 15 minutes
Cooking Time: 8 minutes
Servings: 4
Ingredients:

- 10 oz. mixed oriental mushrooms, such as oyster, shiitake and enoki, cleaned and sliced

- 7 oz. thin rice noodles, cooked according to packet instructions and drained
- 2 garlic cloves, minced
- 1 fresh red chili
- 7 oz. courgettes, sliced
- 6 spring onions, reserving the green part
- 1 teaspoon corn flour
- 1 tablespoon agave syrup
- 1 teaspoon sesame oil
- 100g baby spinach, chopped
- Hot chili sauce, to serve
- 2(1-inch) pieces of ginger
- ½ bunch fresh coriander, chopped
- 4 tablespoons vegetable oil
- 2 tablespoons low-salt soy sauce
- ½ tablespoon rice wine
- 2 limes, to serve

Directions:

1. Heat sesame oil over high heat in a large wok and add the mushrooms.
2. Sauté for about 4 minutes and add garlic, chili, ginger, courgette, coriander stalks and the white part of the spring onions.
3. Sauté for about 3 minutes until softened and lightly golden.
4. Meanwhile, combine the corn flour and 2 tablespoons of water in a bowl.
5. Add soy sauce, agave syrup, sesame oil and rice wine to the corn flour mixture.
6. Put this mixture in the pan to the veggie mixture and cook for about 3 minutes until thickened.
7. Add the spinach and noodles and mix well.
8. Stir in the coriander leaves and top with lime wedges, hot

chili sauce and reserved spring onions to serve.

Nutrition: Calories: 314 Fat: 22g Protein: 26g Carbs: 8g Fiber: 0.3g

Vegetable Penne Pasta

Preparation Time: 15 minutes
Cooking Time: 20 minutes
Servings: 6
Ingredients:

- ½ large onion, chopped
- 2 celery sticks, chopped
- ½ tablespoon ginger paste
- ½ cup green bell pepper
- 1½ tablespoons soy sauce
- ½ teaspoon parsley
- Salt and black pepper, to taste
- ½ pound penne pasta, cooked
- 2 large carrots, diced
- ½ small leek, chopped
- 1 tablespoon olive oil
- ½ teaspoon garlic paste
- ½ tablespoon Worcester sauce
- ½ teaspoon coriander
- 1 cup water

Directions:

1. Heat olive oil in a wok on medium heat and add onions, garlic and ginger paste.
2. Sauté for about 3 minutes and stir in all bell pepper, celery sticks, carrots and leek.
3. Sauté for about 5 minutes and add remaining ingredients except for pasta.
4. Cover the lid and cook for about 12 minutes.
5. Stir in the cooked pasta and dish out to serve warm.

Nutrition: Calories: 385 Fat: 29g Protein: 26g Carbs: 12g Fiber: 1g

Spiced Tomato Brown Rice

Preparation Time: 10 minutes

Cooking Time: 15 minutes

Servings: 4 to 6

Ingredients:

- 1 onion, diced
- 1 green bell pepper, diced
- 3 cloves garlic, minced
- ¼ cup water
- 15 to 16oz. (425 to 454g) tomatoes, chopped
- 1 tablespoon chili powder
- 2 teaspoons ground cumin
- 1 teaspoon dried basil
- ½ teaspoon Parsley Patch seasoning, general blend
- ¼ teaspoon cayenne
- 2 cups cooked brown rice

Directions:

1. Combine the onion, green pepper, garlic and water in a saucepan over medium heat.
2. Cook for about 5 minutes, stirring constantly, or until softened.
3. Add the tomatoes and seasonings.
4. Cook for another 5 minutes.
5. Stir in the cooked rice.
6. Cook for another 5 minutes to allow the flavors to blend.
7. Serve immediately.

Nutrition: Calories: 107 Fat: 1.1g Carbs: 21.1g Protein: 3.2g Fiber: 2.9g

Noodle and Rice Pilaf

Preparation Time: 5 minutes

Cooking Time: 33 to 44 minutes

Servings: 6 to 8

Ingredients:

- 1 cup whole-wheat noodles, broken into
- 1/8 inch pieces

- 2 cups long-grain brown rice
- 6½ cups low-sodium vegetable broth
- 1 teaspoon ground cumin
- ½ teaspoon dried oregano

Directions:

1. Combine the noodles and rice in a saucepan over medium heat and cook for 3 to 4 minutes, or until they begin to smell toasted.
2. Stir in the vegetable broth, cumin and oregano.
3. Bring to a boil.
4. Reduce the heat to medium-low.
5. Cover and cook for 30 to 40 minutes, or until all water is absorbed.

Nutrition: Calories: 287 Fat: 2.5g Carbs: 58.1g Protein: 7.9g Fiber: 5.0g

Easy Millet Loaf

Preparation Time: 5 minutes
Cooking Time: 1 hour 15 minutes
Servings: 4
Ingredients:

- 1¼ cups millet
- 4 cups unsweetened tomato juice
- 1 medium onion, chopped
- 1 to 2 cloves garlic
- ½ teaspoon dried sage
- ½ teaspoon dried basil
- ½ teaspoon poultry seasoning

Directions:

1. Preheat the oven to 350°F.
2. Place the millet in a large bowl.
3. Place the remaining ingredients in a blender and pulse until smooth.
4. Add to the bowl with the millet and mix well.

5. Pour the mixture into a shallow casserole dish.
6. Cover and bake in the oven for 1¼ hours, or until set.
7. Serve warm.

Nutrition: Calories: 315 Fat: 3.4g Carbs: 61.6g Protein: 10.2g Fiber: 9.6g

Walnut-Oat Burgers

Preparation Time: 5 minutes
Cooking Time: 20 to 30 minutes
Servings: 6 to 8
Ingredients:

- 1 medium onion, finely chopped
- 2 cups rolled oats
- 2 cups unsweetened low-Fat: soy milk
- 1 cup finely chopped walnuts
- 1 tablespoon soy sauce
- ½ teaspoon dried sage
- ½ teaspoon garlic powder
- ½ teaspoon onion powder
- ½ teaspoon dried thyme
- ¼ teaspoon dried marjoram

Directions:

1. Stir together all the ingredients in a large bowl.
2. Let rest for 20 minutes.
3. Form the mixture into six or eight patties.
4. Cook the patties on a nonstick griddle over medium heat for 20 to 30 minutes, or until browned on each side.
5. Serve warm.

Nutrition: Calories: 341 Fat: 13.9g Carbs: 42.4g Protein: 13.9g Fiber: 6.8g

Spicy Beans and Rice

Preparation Time: 5 minutes
Cooking Time: 45 minutes
Servings: 4 to 6
Ingredients:

- 1½ cups long-grain brown rice
- 1 (19-oz.) can kidney beans, rinsed and drained
- 2 cups chopped onion
- 1 cup mild salsa
- 1 teaspoon ground cumin
- 16 oz. tomatoes, chopped
- 3 cups water

Directions:

1. In a pot, bring the water to a boil.
2. Stir in the rice.
3. Bring to a boil again and stir in the remaining ingredients, except for the tomatoes.
4. Return to a boil.
5. Reduce the heat to low.
6. Cover and simmer for 45 minutes.
7. Remove from the heat and stir in the tomatoes.
8. Let sit for 5 minutes, covered.

Nutrition: Calories: 386 Fat: 7.1g Carbs: 71.1g Protein: 11.1g Fiber: 5.8g

DINNER

Alfredo Pasta With Cherry Tomatoes

Preparation Time: 15-30 minutes
Cooking Time: 20 minutes
Servings: 4
Ingredients:
- 2 cups almond milk
- 1 ½ cups vegetable broth
- 3 tbsp plant butter
- 1 large garlic clove, minced
- 16 oz whole-wheat fettuccine
- ½ cup coconut cream
- ¼ cup halved cherry tomatoes
- ¾ cup grated plant-based Parmesan cheese
- Salt and black pepper to taste
- Chopped fresh parsley to garnish

Directions:
1. Bring almond milk, vegetable broth, butter, and garlic to a boil in a large pot, 5 minutes.
2. Mix in the fettuccine and cook until tender, while frequently tossing around 10 minutes.
3. Mix in coconut cream, tomatoes, plant Parmesan cheese, salt, and pepper.
4. Cook for 3 minutes or until the cheese melts.
5. Garnish with some parsley and serve warm.

Nutrition: Calories 698 kcal Fats 26. 1g Carbs 101. 8g Protein 22. 6g

Tempeh Tetrazzini With Garden Peas

Preparation Time: 15-30 minutes
Cooking Time: 50 minutes
Servings: 4
Ingredients:
- 16 oz whole-wheat bow-tie pasta
- 2 tbsp olive oil, divided
- 2/3 lb tempeh, cut into 1-inch cubes
- Salt and black pepper to taste
- 1 medium yellow onion, chopped
- ½ cup sliced white mushrooms
- 2 tbsp whole-wheat flour
- ¼ cup white wine

- ¾ cup vegetable stock
- ¼ cup oats milk
- 2 tsp chopped fresh thyme
- ¼ cup chopped cauliflower
- ½ cup grated plant-based Parmesan cheese
- 3 tbsp whole-wheat breadcrumbs

Directions:
1. Cook the pasta in 8 cups of slightly salted water for 10 minutes or until al dente.
2. Drain and set aside.
3. Preheat the oven to 375 F.
4. Heat the 1 tbsp of olive oil in a skillet over medium heat, season the tempeh with salt, pepper, and cook until golden brown all around.
5. Mix in onion, mushrooms, and cook until softened, 5 minutes.
6. Stir in flour and cook for 1 more minute.
7. Mix in wine and add two-thirds of the vegetable stock.
8. Cook for 2 minutes while occasionally stirring and then add milk; continue cooking until the sauce thickens, 4 minutes.
9. Season with the thyme, salt, black pepper, and half of the Parmesan cheese.
10. Once the cheese melts, turn the heat off and allow cooling.
11. Add the rest of the vegetable stock and cauliflower to a food processor and blend until smooth. Pour the mixture into a bowl, pour in the sauce, and mix in pasta until combined.
12. Grease a 2 quarts glass baking dish with cooking spray and spread the mixture in the baking dish.
13. Drizzle the remaining olive oil on top, breadcrumbs, some more thyme, and the remaining cheese.
14. Bake until the cheese melts and is golden brown on top, 30 minutes.
15. Remove the dish from the oven, allow cooling for 3 minutes, and serve.

Nutrition: Calories 799 kcal Fats 57. 7g Carbs 54. 3g Protein 27g

Tomato, Kale, and White Bean Skillet

Preparation Time: 10 minutes
Cooking Time: 10 minutes

Servings: 4
Ingredients:

- 30 ounces cooked cannellini beans
- 3. 5 ounces sun-dried tomatoes, packed in oil, chopped
- 6 ounces kale, chopped
- 1 teaspoon minced garlic
- 1/4 teaspoon ground black pepper
- 1/4 teaspoon salt
- 1/2 tablespoon dried basil
- 1/8 teaspoon red pepper flakes
- 1 tablespoon apple cider vinegar
- 1 tablespoon olive oil
- 2 tablespoons oil from sun-dried tomatoes

Directions:

1. Prepare the dressing and for this, place basil, black pepper, salt, vinegar, and red pepper flakes in a small bowl, add oil from sun-dried tomatoes and whisk until combined.
2. Take a skillet pan, place it over medium heat, add olive oil and when hot, add garlic and cook for 1 minute until fragrant.
3. Add kale, splash with some water and cook for 3 minutes until kale leaves have wilted.
4. Add tomatoes and beans, stir well and cook for 3 minutes until heated.
5. Remove pan from heat, drizzle with the prepared dressing, toss until mixed and serve.

Nutrition: Calories: 264 Cal Fat: 12 g Carbs: 38 g Protein: 9 g Fiber: 13 g

Chard Wraps With Millet

Preparation Time: 25 minutes
Cooking Time: 0 minute
Servings: 4
Ingredients:

- 1 carrot, cut into ribbons
- 1/2 cup millet, cooked
- 1/2 of a large cucumber, cut into ribbons
- 1/2 cup chickpeas, cooked
- 1 cup sliced cabbage
- 1/3 cup hummus
- Mint leaves as needed for topping Hemp seeds as needed for topping

- 1 bunch of Swiss rainbow chard

Directions:
1. Spread hummus on one side of the chard, place some millet, vegetables, and chickpeas on it, sprinkle with some mint leaves and hemp seeds and wrap it like a burrito.
2. Serve straight away.

Nutrition: Calories: 152 Cal Fat: 4. 5 g Carbs: 25 g Protein: 3. 5 g Fiber: 2. 4 g

Quinoa Meatballs

Preparation Time: 10 minutes
Cooking Time: 35 minutes
Servings: 4
Ingredients:
- 1 cup quinoa, cooked
- 1 tablespoon flax meal
- 1 cup diced white onion
- 1 ½ teaspoon minced garlic
- 1/2 teaspoon salt
- 1 teaspoon dried oregano
- 1 teaspoon lemon zest
- 1 teaspoon paprika
- 1 teaspoon dried basil
- 3 tablespoons water
- 2 tablespoons olive oil

- 1 cup grated vegan mozzarella cheese Marinara sauce as needed for serving

Directions:
1. Place flax meal in a bowl, stir in water, and set aside until required.
2. Take a large skillet pan, place it over medium heat, add 1 tablespoon oil and when hot, add onion and cook for 2 minutes.
3. Stir in all the spices and herbs, then stir in quinoa until combined and cook for 2 minutes.
4. Transfer quinoa mixture in a bowl, add flax meal mixture, lemon zest, and cheese, stir until well mixed and then shape the mixture into twelve 1 ½ inch balls.
5. Arrange balls on a baking sheet lined with parchment paper, refrigerate the balls for 30
6. minutes and then bake for 20 minutes at 400 degrees F.
7. Serve balls with marinara sauce.

Nutrition: Calories: 100 Cal Fat: 100 g Carbs: 100 g Protein: 100 g Fiber: 100 g

Cauliflower Sushi

Preparation Time: 30 minutes
Cooking Time: 3-30 minutes
Servings: 4
 Ingredients:
- Sushi Base:
- 6 cups cauliflower florets
- ½ cup vegan cheese
- 1 medium spring onion, diced
- 4 nori sheets
- Sea salt and pepper to taste
- 1 tbsp. rice vinegar or sushi vinegar
- 1 medium garlic clove, minced
- Filling:
- 1 medium Hass avocado, peeled, sliced
- ½ medium cucumber, skinned, sliced
- 4 asparagus spears
- A handful of enoki mushrooms

Directions:
1. Put the cauliflower florets in a food processor or blender.
2. Pulse the florets into a rice-like substance.
3. When using ready-made cauliflower rice, add this to the blender.
4. Add the vegan cheese, spring onions, and vinegar to the food processor or blender.
5. Top these ingredients with salt and pepper to taste, and pulse everything into a chunky mixture.
6. Make sure not to turn the ingredients into a puree by pulsing too long.
7. Taste and add more vinegar, salt, or pepper to taste.
8. Add the optional minced garlic clove to the blender and pulse again for a few seconds.
9. Lay the nori sheets and spread the cauliflower rice mixture out evenly between the sheets.
10. Make sure to leave at least 2 inches of the top and bottom edges empty.
11. Place one or more combinations of multiple filling ingredients along the center of the spreadout rice mixture.
12. Experiment with different ingredients per nori sheet for the best flavor.
13. Roll up each nori sheet tightly. (Using a sushi mat will make this easier.)

14. Either serve the sushi as a nori roll or, slice each roll up into sushi pieces.
15. Serve right away with a small amount of wasabi, pickled ginger, and soy sauce!

Nutrition: Calories 189 Carbohydrates 7. 6 g Fats 14. 4 g Protein

Pinwheel Greens

Preparation Time: 5 minutes
Cooking Time: 1 minute
Servings: 16

Ingredients:
- ½ cup of water
- 4 tablespoons white vinegar
- 3 tablespoons lemon juice
- 3 tablespoons tahini paste
- 1 clove garlic, minced
- Salt and pepper to taste
- Canned artichokes, drained, thinly sliced
- Cherry tomatoes, thinly sliced
- Olives, thinly sliced
- Lettuce or baby spinach
- Tortillas Directions: • In a bowl, combine the water, vinegar, lemon juice, and Tahini paste; whisk together until smooth.
- Add the garlic, salt, and pepper to taste; whisk to combine. Set the bowl aside.
- Lay a tortilla on a flat surface and spread with one tablespoon of the sauce.
- Lay some lettuce or spinach slices on top, then scatter some artichoke, tomato, and olive slices on top.
- Tightly roll the tortilla and fold in the sides. Cut the ends off and then slice into four or five pinwheels.
Nutrition:
- Calories 322 Carbohydrates 5 g Fats 4 g Protein 30 g

Guacamole Rice and Bean Burritos

Preparation Time: 10 minutes
Cooking Time: 15 minutes
Servings: 8
Ingredients:
- 2 16-ounce cans fat-free refried beans
- 6 tortillas
- 2 cups cooked rice
- ½ cup of salsa
- 1 tablespoon olive oil
- 1 bunch green onions, chopped
- 2 bell peppers, finely chopped

- Guacamole

Directions:
1. Preheat the oven to 375°F.
2. Dump the refried beans into a saucepan and place over medium heat to warm.
3. Heat the tortillas and lay them out on a flat surface.
4. Spoon the beans in a long mound that runs across the tortilla, just a little off from the center.
5. Spoon some rice and salsa over the beans; add the green pepper and onions to taste, along with any other finely chopped vegetables you like.
6. Fold over the shortest edge of the plain tortilla and roll it up, folding in the sides as you go.
7. Place each burrito, seam side down, on a baking sheet sprayed with a non-stick spray.
8. Brush with olive oil and bake for 15 minutes.
9. Serve with guacamole.

Nutrition: Calories 290 Carbohydrates 49 g Fats 6 g Protein 9 g

Ricotta Basil Pinwheels

Preparation Time: 10 minutes
Cooking Time: 3-30 minutes
Servings: 4
Ingredients:
- ½ cup unsalted cashews
- Water
- 7 ounces firm tofu, cut into pieces
- ¼ cup almond milk
- 1 teaspoon white wine vinegar
- 1 clove garlic, smashed
- 20 to 25 fresh basil leaves
- Salt and pepper to taste
- 8 tortillas
- 7 ounces fresh spinach
- ½ cup black olives, sliced
- 2 to 3 tomatoes, cut into small pieces

Directions:
1. Soak the cashews for 30 minutes in enough water to cover them.
2. Drain them well and pat them dry with paper towels.
3. Place the cashews in a blender along with the tofu, almond milk, vinegar, garlic,

basil leaves, salt, and pepper to taste.

4. Blend until smooth and creamy.
5. Spread the resulting mixture on the eight tortillas, dividing it equally.
6. Top with spinach leaves, olives, and tomatoes.
7. Tightly roll each loaded tortilla.
8. Cut off the ends with a sharp knife and slice into four or five pinwheels.

Nutrition: Calories 236 Carbohydrates 6. 1 g Fats 21. 6 g Protein 4. 2 g

Delicious Sloppy Joes With No Meat

Preparation Time: 6 minutes
Cooking Time: 5 minutes
Servings: 4
Ingredients:
- 5 tablespoons vegetable stock
- 2 stalks celery, diced
- 1 small onion, diced
- 1 small red bell pepper, diced
- 1 teaspoon garlic powder
- 1 teaspoon chili powder
- 1 teaspoon ground cumin
- 1 teaspoon salt
- 1 cup cooked bulgur wheat
- 1 cup red lentils
- 1 15-ounce can tomato sauce
- 4 tablespoons tomato paste
- 3½ cups water
- 2 teaspoons balsamic vinegar
- 1 tablespoon Hoisin sauce

Directions:
1. In a Dutch oven, heat the vegetable stock and add the celery, onion, and bell pepper.
2. Sauté until vegetables are soft, about five minutes.
3. Add the garlic powder, chili powder, cumin, and salt and mix in.
4. Add the bulgur wheat, lentils, tomato sauce, tomato paste, water, vinegar, and Hoisin sauce.
5. Stir and bring to a boil.
6. Turn the heat down to a simmer and cook uncovered for 30 minutes.
7. Stir occasionally to prevent sticking and scorching.
8. Taste to see if the lentils are tender.
9. When the lentils are done, serve on buns.

Nutrition: Calories 451 Fats 10 g Carbohydrates 61 g Protein 27 g

Beauty School Ginger Cucumbers

Preparation Time: 10 minutes
Cooking Time: 45 minutes
Servings: 14
Ingredients:
- 1 sliced cucumber
- 3 tsp. rice wine vinegar
- 1 ½ tbsp. sugar
- 1 tsp. minced ginger

Directions:
1. Place all together the ingredients in a mixing bowl, and toss the ingredients well.
2. Enjoy!

Nutrition: Calories: 10 kcal
Protein: 0.46 g Fat: 0.43 g
Carbohydrates: 0.89 g

Exotic Butternut Squash and Chickpea Curry

Preparation Time: 20 minutes
Cooking Time: 6 hours
Servings: 8
Ingredients:
- 1 1/2 cups of shelled peas
- 1 1/2 cups of chickpeas, uncooked and rinsed
- 2 1/2 cups of diced butternut squash
- 12 ounce of chopped spinach
- 2 large tomatoes, diced
- 1 small white onion, peeled and chopped
- 1 teaspoon of minced garlic
- 1 teaspoon of salt
- 3 tablespoons of curry powder
- 14-ounce of coconut milk
- 3 cups of vegetable broth
- 1/4 cup of chopped cilantro

Directions:
- Using a 6-quarts slow cooker, place all the ingredients into it except for the spinach and peas.
- Cover the top, plug in the slow cooker; adjust the cooking time to 6 hours, and cook on the high heat setting or until the chickpeas get tender.
- 30 minutes to ending your cooking, add the peas and spinach to the slow cooker and cook for the remaining 30 minutes.
- Stir to check the sauce; if the sauce is runny, stir in a mixture of a 1 tbsp.

- Cornstarch mixed with 2 tbsp.
- Water.
- Serve with boiled rice.

Nutrition: Calories: 774 kcal Protein: 3.71 g Fat: 83.25 g Carbohydrates: 12.64 g

Sage Walnuts and Radishes

Preparation Time: 10 minutes
Cooking Time: 10 minutes
Servings: 6
Ingredients:
- 2 tablespoons olive oil
- 5 celery ribs, chopped
- 3 spring onions, chopped
- ½ pound radishes, halved juice of 1 lime Zest of 1 lime, grated
- 8 ounces walnuts, chopped
- A pinch of black pepper
- 3 tablespoons sage, chopped

Directions:
1. Heat up a pan with the oil over medium heat, add celery and spring onion, stir and cook for 5 minutes.

2. Add the rest of the ingredients, toss, cook for another 5 minutes, divide into bowls and serve.

Nutrition: calories 200 fat 7 fiber 5 carbs 9.3 protein 4

Garlic Zucchini and Cauliflower

Preparation Time: 10 minutes
Cooking Time: 20 minutes
Servings: 4
Ingredients:
- 4 zucchinis, cut into medium fries
- 1 cup cauliflower florets
- 1 tablespoon capers, drained Juice of ½ lemon
- A pinch of salt and black pepper
- ½ teaspoon chili powder
- 1 tablespoon olive oil
- ¼ teaspoon garlic powder

Directions:
1. Spread the zucchini fries on a lined baking sheet, add the rest of the ingredients, toss, introduce in the oven, bake at 400 degrees F for 20

minutes, divide between plates and serve.

Nutrition: calories 185 fat 3 fiber 2 carbs 6.5 protein 8

Garlic Beans

Preparation Time: 10 minutes
Cooking Time: 10 minutes
Servings: 4
Ingredients:
- Juice of 1 lemon
- Zest of 1 lemon, grated
- 2 tablespoons avocado oil
- 4 garlic cloves, minced
- ½ teaspoon turmeric powder
- 1 teaspoon garam masala
- 1 red onion, sliced
- 1 yellow bell pepper, sliced
- 10 ounces green beans, halved
- A pinch of black pepper

Directions:
1. Heat up a pan with the oil over medium-high heat, add the garlic and onion and cook for 2 minutes.
2. Add green beans and the other ingredients, toss, cook for 8 minutes, divide between plates and serve.

Nutrition: calories 180 fat 10 fiber 6 carbs 13 protein 8

Dinner Lentil and Chickpea Salad

Preparation time: 10 minutes
Cooking time: 0 minute
Servings: 4
Ingredients:
For the Lemon Dressing:
- ¼ cup lemon juice
- 2 tablespoons olive oil
- 1 teaspoon Dijon mustard
- 1 teaspoon honey or maple syrup
- ½ teaspoon minced garlic
- ¼ teaspoon of sea salt
- ¼ teaspoon ground black pepper

For the Salad:
- 2 cups French green lentils, cooked
- 1 ½ cups cooked chickpeas
- 1 medium avocado, pitted, sliced
- 1 big bunch of radishes, chopped
- ¼ cup chopped mint and dill

- Crumbled vegan feta cheese as needed

Directions:
1. Prepare the dressing and for this, place all of its ingredients in a bowl and whisk until combined.
2. Take a large bowl, place all the ingredients for the salad in it, drizzle with the dressing and toss until combined.
3. Serve straight away.

Nutrition: Calories: 311 kcal Protein: 19.94 g Fat: 21.02 g Carbohydrates: 15.55 g

Roasted Carrots with Farro, and Chickpeas

Preparation time: 10 minutes
Cooking time: 35 minutes
Servings: 4
Ingredients:
For the Chickpeas and Farro:
- 1 cup farro, cooked
- 1 ½ cups cooked chickpeas
- ½ teaspoon minced garlic
- 1 teaspoon lemon juice
- ½ teaspoon salt
- 1 teaspoon olive oil

For the Roasted Carrots:
- 1 pound heirloom carrots, scrubbed
- ½ teaspoon ground black pepper
- ¼ teaspoon ground cumin
- 1 teaspoon salt
- 1 tablespoon olive oil

For the Spiced Pepitas:
- 3 tablespoons green pumpkin seeds
- 1/8 teaspoon salt
- 1/8 teaspoon red chili powder
- 1/8 teaspoon cumin
- ½ teaspoon olive oil

For the Crème Fraiche:
- 1 tablespoon chopped parsley
- 1/3 cup vegan crème fraîche
- ¼ teaspoon ground black pepper
- 1/3 teaspoon salt
- 2 teaspoons water

For the Garnish:
- 1 more tablespoon chopped parsley

Directions:
1. Prepare chickpeas and farro and for this, place all of its ingredients in a bowl and toss until combined.

2. Prepare the carrots and for this, arrange them on a baking sheet lined with parchment paper, drizzle with oil, sprinkle with the seasoning, toss until coated, and bake for 35 minutes until roasted and fork-tender, turning halfway.

3. Meanwhile, prepare pepitas and for this, take a skillet pan, place it over medium heat, add oil and when hot, add remaining ingredients in it and cook for 3 minutes until seeds are golden on the edges, set aside, and let it cool.

4. Prepare the crème Fraiche and for this, place all its ingredients in a bowl and whisk until combined.

5. Top chickpeas and farro with carrots, drizzle with crème Fraiche, sprinkle with pepitas and parsley and then serve.

Nutrition: Calories: 321 kcal Protein: 19.94 g Fat: 24.02 g Carbohydrates: 15.75 g

Spaghetti Squash Burrito Bowls

Preparation time: 10 minutes
Cooking time: 60 minutes
Servings: 4
Ingredients:
For the Spaghetti Squash:
- 2 medium spaghetti squash , halved, deseeded
- 2 tablespoons olive oil
- 1 teaspoon salt
- ½ teaspoon ground black pepper

For the Slaw:
- 1/3 cup chopped green onions
- 2 cups chopped purple cabbage
- 1/3 cup chopped cilantro
- 15 ounces cooked black beans
- 1 medium red bell pepper, cored, chopped
- ¼ teaspoon salt 1 teaspoon olive oil
- 2 tablespoons lime juice

For the Salsa Verde:
- 1 avocado, pitted, diced
- ½ teaspoon minced garlic
- ¾ cup salsa verde
- 1/3 cup cilantro
- 1 tablespoon lime juice

Directions:

1. Prepare the squash and for this, place squash halves on a baking sheet lined with parchment paper, rub them with oil, season with salt and black pepper and bake for 60 minutes until roasted and fork-tender.
2. Meanwhile, place the slaw and for this, place all of its ingredients in a bowl and toss until combined.
3. Prepare the salsa, and for this, place all of its ingredients in a food processor and pulse until smooth.
4. When squash has baked, fluff its flesh with a fork, then top with slaw and salsa and serve.

Nutrition: Calories: 381 kcal Protein: 29.94 g Fat: 21502 g Carbohydrates:30.55 g

Spanish Rice

Preparation time: 5 minutes
Cooking time: 40 minutes
Servings: 4

Ingredients:

- 1/2 of medium green bell pepper, chopped
- 1 medium white onion, peeled, chopped
- 10 ounces diced tomatoes with green chilies
- 1 teaspoon salt
- 2 teaspoons red chili powder
- 1 cup white rice
- 2 tablespoons olive oil
- 2 cups of water

Directions:

1. Take a large skillet pan, place it over medium heat, add oil and when hot, add onion, pepper, and rice, and cook for 10 minutes.
2. Then add remaining ingredients, stir until mixed, bring the mixture to a boil, then simmer over medium-low heat for 30 minutes until cooked and most of the liquid has absorbed.
3. Serve straight away.

Nutrition: Calories: 310 kcal Protein: 19.90 g Fat: 21.0 g Carbohydrates: 15.4 g

Black Beans and Rice

Preparation time: 10 minutes
Cooking time: 30 minutes
Servings: 4
Ingredients:

- 3/4 cup white rice
- 1 medium white onion, peeled, chopped
- 3 1/2 cups cooked black beans
- 1 teaspoon minced garlic
- 1/4 teaspoon cayenne pepper
- 1 teaspoon ground cumin
- 1 teaspoon olive oil
- 1 1/2 cups vegetable broth

Directions:

1. Take a large pot over medium-high heat, add oil and when hot, add onion and garlic and cook for 4 minutes until saute.
2. Then stir in rice, cook for 2 minutes, pour in the broth, bring it to a boil, switch heat to the low level and cook for 20 minutes until tender.
3. Stir in remaining ingredients, cook for 2 minutes, and then serve straight away.

Nutrition: Calories: 311 kcal
Protein: 19.94 g Fat: 21.02 g
Carbohydrates: 15.55 g

Sweet Potato and White Bean Skillet

Preparation time: 10 minutes
Cooking time: 45 minutes
Servings: 4
Ingredients:

- 1 large bunch of kale, chopped
- 2 large sweet potatoes, peeled,
- ¼-inch cubes
- 12 ounces cannellini beans
- 1 small onion, peeled, diced
- 1/8 teaspoon red pepper flakes
- 1 teaspoon salt
- 1 teaspoon cumin
- ½ teaspoon ground black pepper
- 1 teaspoon curry powder
- 1 1/2 tablespoons coconut oil
- 6 ounces coconut milk, unsweetened

Directions:

1. Take a large skillet pan, place it over medium heat, add ½ tablespoon oil and when it melts, add onion and cook for 5 minutes.
2. Then stir in sweet potatoes, stir well, cook for 5 minutes, then season with all the

spices, cook for 1 minute and remove the pan from heat.

3. Take another pan, add remaining oil in it, place it over medium heat and when oil melts, add kale, season with some salt and black pepper, stir well, pour in the milk and cook for 15 minutes until tender.
4. Then add beans, beans, and red pepper, stir until mixed and cook for 5 minutes until hot.
5. Serve straight away.

Nutrition: Calories 369 kcal Fats 12. 7g Carbs 52. 7g Protein 15. 6g

Black Bean Burgers

Preparation time: 25 Minutes
Cooking time: 10 minutes
Serves: 6
Ingredients:
- 1 Onion, Diced
- ½ Cup Corn Nibs
- 2 Cloves Garlic, Minced
- ½ Teaspoon Oregano, Dried
- ½ Cup Flour

- 1 Jalapeno Pepper, Small
- 2 Cups Black Beans, Mashed & Canned
- ¼ Cup Breadcrumbs (Vegan)
- 2 Teaspoons Parsley, Minced
- ¼ Teaspoon Cumin
- 1 Tablespoon Olive Oil
- 2 Teaspoons Chili Powder
- ½ Red Pepper, Diced
- Sea Salt to Taste

Directions:
1. Set your flour on a plate, and then get out your garlic, onion, peppers and oregano, throwing it in a pan.
2. Cook over medium-high heat, and then cook until the onions are translucent.
3. Place the peppers in, and sauté until tender.
4. Cook for two minutes, and then set it to the side.
5. Use a potato masher to mash your black beans, and then stir in the vegetables, cumin, breadcrumbs, parsley, salt and chili powder, and then divide it into six patties.
6. Coat each side, and then cook until it's fried on each side.

Nutrition: Calories 359 kcal Fats 12. 7g Carbs 60. 7g Protein 15. 6g

Hearty Black Lentil Curry

Preparation time: 6 hours and 35 minutes
Cooking time: 6 hours
Servings: 4
Ingredients:

- 1 cup of black lentils, rinsed and soaked overnight
- 14 ounce of chopped tomatoes
- 2 large white onions, peeled and sliced
- 1 1/2 teaspoon of minced garlic
- 1 teaspoon of grated ginger
- 1 red chili
- 1 teaspoon of salt
- 1/4 teaspoon of red chili powder
- 1 teaspoon of paprika
- 1 teaspoon of ground turmeric
- 2 teaspoons of ground cumin
- 2 teaspoons of ground coriander
- 1/2 cup of chopped coriander
- 4-ounce of vegetarian butter
- 4 fluid of ounce water
- 2 fluid of ounce vegetarian double cream

Directions:

1. Place a large pan over an average heat, add butter and let heat until melt.
2. Add the onion along with garlic and ginger and let cook for 10 to 15 minutes or until onions are caramelized.
3. Then stir in salt, red chili powder, paprika, turmeric, cumin, ground coriander, and water.
4. Transfer this mixture to a 6-quarts slow cooker and add tomatoes and red chili.
5. Drain lentils, add to slow cooker and stir until just mix.
6. Plug in slow cooker; adjust cooking time to 6 hours and let cook on low heat setting.
7. When the lentils are done, stir in cream and adjust the seasoning.
8. Serve with boiled rice or whole wheat bread.

Nutrition: calories 270; Total fat: 9g; Protein: 15g; Sodium: 158mg; Fiber: 12g

Smoky Red Beans and Rice

Preparation time: 10 minutes
Cooking time: 5 hours
Servings: 6
Ingredients:

- 30 ounce of cooked red beans
- 1 cup of brown rice, uncooked
- 1 cup of chopped green pepper
- 1 cup of chopped celery
- 1 cup of chopped white onion
- 1 1/2 teaspoon of minced garlic
- 1/2 teaspoon of salt
- 1/4 teaspoon of cayenne pepper
- 1 teaspoon of smoked paprika
- 2 teaspoons of dried thyme
- 1 bay leaf 2
- 1/3 cups of vegetable broth

Directions:

1. Using a 6-quarts slow cooker place all the ingredients except for the rice, salt and cayenne pepper.
2. Stir until it mixes properly and then cover the top.
3. Plug in the slow cooker; adjust the cooking time to 4 hours and let it steam on a low heat setting.
4. Then pour in and stir the rice, salt, cayenne pepper and continue cooking for an additional 2 hours at a high heat setting.
5. Serve straight away.

Nutrition: calories 280; Total fat: 7g; Protein: 13g; Sodium: 168mg; Fiber: 12g

Creamy Artichoke Soup

Preparation time: 5 minutes
Cooking time: 40 minutes
Servings: 4
Ingredients:

- 1 can artichoke hearts, drained
- 3 cups vegetable broth
- 2 tbsp lemon juice
- 1 small onion, finely cut
- 2 cloves garlic, crushed
- 3 tbsp olive oil
- 2 tbsp flour
- ½ cup vegan cream

Directions:

1. Gently sauté the onion and garlic in some olive oil.
2. Add the flour, whisking constantly, and then add the

hot vegetable broth slowly, while still whisking.

3. Cook for about 5 minutes.
4. Blend the artichoke, lemon juice, salt and pepper until smooth.
5. Add the puree to the broth mix, stir well, and then stir in the cream.
6. Cook until heated through.
7. Garnish with a swirl of vegan cream or a sliver of artichoke.
8. Super Rad-ish

Nutrition: Calories: 544; Protein: 23g; Total fat: 17g; Saturated fat: 3g; Carbohydrates: 83g; Fiber: 13g

Sweet Potato and Cauliflower Salad

Preparation Time: 10 minutes
Cooking time: 30 minutes
Servings: 8
Ingredients:
For the Salad:

- 1 1/2 pound small sweet potatoes, peeled, cut into ½-inch wedges
- 2/3 cup pomegranate seeds
- 1 small head of cauliflower, cut into florets

- 8 cups mixed lettuces
- 1/2 teaspoon salt
- 1/4 teaspoon ground black pepper
- 3 tablespoons olive oil, divided

For the Dressing:

- 4 tablespoons olive oil, divided
- 1/2 teaspoon salt
- 1/4 teaspoon ground black pepper
- 3 tablespoons apple cider vinegar

Direction:

1. Take a baking dish, place all the vegetables for the salad on it, drizzle with oil, season with salt and black pepper, stir until well coated, then bake for 30 minutes at 425 degrees F until roasted.
2. In the meantime, prepare the dressing and for this put all his shopping list: in a bowl and beat until combined.
3. When the vegetables are roasted, let them cool for 10 minutes, then place them in a large bowl along with the rest of the shopping list: for the salad, sprinkle with the dressing and stir until covered.

4. Serve immediately.

Nutrition: Calories: 330 Cal Fat: 14 g Carbs: 33 g Protein: 9.8 g Fiber: 18 g

Wild Rice & Millet Croquettes

Preparation Time: 5 Minutes
Cooking Time: 20 Minutes
Serves: 4 To 6
Ingredients:

- ¾ cup cooked millet
- ½ cup cooked wild rice
- 3 tablespoons extra-virgin olive oil
- ¼ cup minced onion
- 1 celery rib, finely minced
- ¼ cup finely shredded carrot
- ⅓ cup all-purpose flour
- ¼ cup chopped fresh parsley
- 2 teaspoons dried dillweed
- Salt and freshly ground black pepper

Direction:

1. Place the cooked millet and wild rice in a large bowl and set aside.
2. In a medium skillet, heat 1 tablespoon of oil over medium heat.
3. Add the onion, celery and carrot.
4. Cover and cook until softened for about 5 minutes.
5. Add the vegetables to the cooked beans.
6. Incorporate the flour, parsley, duckweed, salt and pepper.
7. Mix until well combined.
8. Refrigerate until it cools for about 20 minutes.
9. To cook Use your hands to shape the mixture into small meatballs and set aside.
10. In a large skillet, heat the remaining 2 tablespoons of oil over medium heat.
11. Add the croquettes and cook until golden brown, turning once, for about 8 minutes in total.
12. Serve immediately

Nutrition: Calories: 200; Fat: 2g; Protein: 13g; Carbohydrates: 34g; Fiber: 12g; Sugar: 1g; Sodium: 41mg

Tomato Basil Salad

Preparation Time: 10 minutes

Cooking time: 0 minute
Servings: 4
Instruction:
- 3 tablespoons chopped red onion
- 1 pound tomatoes, chopped
- 10 leaves of basil, cut into ribbons
- 1/4 teaspoon ground black pepper
- 1/2 teaspoon salt
- 2 tablespoons white balsamic vinegar

Direction.
1. Take a large bowl, put the whole shopping list: in it, mix until well blended, then let it rest for 5 minutes.
2. Refrigerate the salad for at least 2 hours and then serve immediately.

Nutrition: Calories: 26 Cal Fat: 0 g Carbs: 5 g Protein: 1 g Fiber: 1 g

Caribbean Rice, Squash, & Peas

Preparation Time: 5 Minutes
Cooking Time: 40 Minutes
Serves: 4
Ingredients:

- 2 tablespoons extra-virgin olive oil
- 1 small yellow onion, chopped
- 2 cups peeled, seeded, and diced butternut or other winter squash
- 3 garlic cloves, minced
- 1 teaspoon dried thyme
- ½ teaspoon ground cumin
- 1½ cups cooked or 1 (15.5-ounce) can black-eyed peas, drained and rinsed
- 1 cup long-grain rice
- 2½ cups hot water
- 2 tablespoons chopped fresh cilantro

Direction:
1. In a large saucepan, heat the oil over medium heat.
2. Add the onion, cover, then cook until softened for about 5 minutes.
3. Add the pumpkin, garlic, thyme and cumin.
4. Cover and cook until the squash has softened for about 10 minutes.
5. Incorporate the peas, rice and water.
6. Bring to a boil, then reduce the heat to low.
7. Cover and simmer until rice is cooked for about 30 minutes.

8. Finish and serve
9. Fluff with a fork and sprinkle with cilantro.
10. Serve immediately.

Nutrition: Calories: 180; Fat: 2g; Protein: 23g; Carbohydrates: 38g; Fiber: 12g; Sugar: 1g; Sodium: 41mg

Lentil Spinach Curry

Preparation Time: 5 Minutes
Cooking Time: 30 Minutes
Serves: 4
Ingredients:

- 1 teaspoon extra-virgin olive oil
- 1 onion, chopped
- ½-inch piece fresh ginger, peeled and minced
- 1 to 2 tablespoons mild curry powder
- 1½ cups dried green or brown lentils
- 2½ cups water or Vegetable Broth
- 1 cup canned diced tomatoes
- 2 to 4 cups finely chopped raw spinach
- ½ cup nondairy milk
- 2 tablespoons soy sauce (optional)
- 1 tablespoon apple cider vinegar or rice vinegar
- 1 teaspoon salt (or 2 teaspoons if omitting soy sauce)

Direction:
1. Heat the olive oil in a large saucepan over medium heat.
2. Add the onion and sauté for about 3 minutes until soft.
3. Add the ginger and cook for 1 minute.
4. Incorporate the curry powder, lentils and water.
5. Bring to a boil, lower the heat and cover the pot.
6. Simmer for about 15-20 minutes until the lentils are soft.
7. Stir in the tomatoes, spinach, milk, soy sauce (if used), vinegar and salt.
8. Simmer for about 3 minutes until heated.
9. If you prefer, use a hand blender to blend it halfway into the pot for a creamier texture and to hide the spinach.
10. Finish and serve Store in an airtight container for 4-5 days in the refrigerator or up to 1 month in the freezer.

Nutrition: Calories: 313; Protein: 21g; Total fat: 3g; Saturated fat: 0g; Carbohydrates: 52g; Fiber: 24g

Green Spinach Kale Soup

Preparation Time: 10 minutes
Cooking Time: 5 minutes
Servings: 6
Ingredients:
- 2 avocados
- 8 oz. spinach
- 8 oz. kale
- 1 fresh lime juice
- 1 cup water
- 3 1/3 cup coconut milk
- 3 oz. olive oil
- 1/4 tsp pepper
- 1 tsp salt

Directions:
1. Heat olive oil in a saucepan over medium heat.
2. Add kale and spinach to the saucepan and sauté for 2-3 minutes.
3. Remove saucepan from heat.
4. Add coconut milk, spices, avocado, and water.
5. Stir well.

6. Puree the soup using an immersion blender until smooth and creamy.
7. Add fresh lime juice and stir well.
8. Serve and enjoy.

Nutrition: Calories: 312 Protein: 9g Fat: 10 Carbs: 22

Cauliflower Asparagus Soup

Preparation Time: 10 minutes
Cooking Time: 30 minutes
Servings: 4
Ingredients:
- 20 asparagus spears, chopped
- 4 cups vegetable stock
- ½ cauliflower head, chopped
- 2 garlic cloves, chopped
- 1 tbsp coconut oil
- Pepper Salt

Directions:
1. Heat coconut oil in a large saucepan over medium heat.
2. Add garlic and sauté until softened.
3. Add cauliflower, vegetable stock, pepper, and salt.
4. Stir well and bring to boil.

5. Reduce heat to low and simmer for 20 minutes.
6. Add chopped asparagus and cook until softened.
7. Puree the soup using an immersion blender until smooth and creamy.
8. Stir well and serve warm.

Nutrition: Calories: 298 Carbs: 26g Protein: 21g Fat: 9g

African Pineapple Peanut Stew

Preparation Time: 10 minutes
Cooking Time: 20 minutes
Servings: 4
Ingredients:
- 4 cups sliced kale
- 1 cup chopped onion
- 1/2 cup peanut butter
- 1 tbsp. hot pepper sauce or 1 tbsp.
- Tabasco sauce 2 minced garlic cloves
- 1/2 cup chopped cilantro
- 2 cups pineapple, undrained, canned & crushed
- 1 tbsp. vegetable oil

Directions:

1. In a saucepan (preferably covered), sauté the garlic and onions in the oil until the onions are lightly browned, approximately 10 minutes, stirring often.
2. Wash the kale, till the time the onions are sauté.
3. Get rid of the stems.
4. Mound the leaves on a cutting surface & slice crosswise into slices (preferably 1" thick).
5. Now put the pineapple and juice to the onions & bring to a simmer.
6. Stir the kale in, cover and simmer until just tender, stirring frequently, approximately 5 minutes.
7. Mix in the hot pepper sauce, peanut butter & simmer for more 5 minutes.
8. Add salt according to your taste.

Nutrition: Calories: 402 Carbs: 7g Protein: 21g Fat: 34g

Cabbage & Beet Stew

Preparation Time: 20 minutes

Cooking Time: 10 minutes
Servings: 4
Ingredients:

- 2 Tablespoons Olive Oil
- 3 Cups Vegetable Broth
- 2 Tablespoons Lemon Juice, Fresh
- ½ Teaspoon Garlic Powder
- ½ Cup Carrots, Shredded
- 2 Cups Cabbage, Shredded
- 1 Cup Beets, Shredded Dill for Garnish
- ½ Teaspoon Onion Powder
- Sea Salt & Black Pepper to Taste

Directions:

1. Heat oil in a pot, and then sauté your vegetables.
2. Pour your broth in, mixing in your seasoning.
3. Simmer until it's cooked through, and then top with dill.

Nutrition: Calories: 263 Carbs: 8g Protein: 20.3g Fat: 24g

Servings: 6
Ingredients:

- 28 oz. can tomatoes
- ¼ cup basil pesto
- ¼ tsp dried basil leaves
- 1 tsp apple cider vinegar
- 2 tbsp erythritol
- ¼ tsp garlic powder
- ½ tsp onion powder
- 2 cups water
- 1 ½ tsp kosher salt

Directions:

1. Add tomatoes, garlic powder, onion powder, water, and salt in a saucepan.
2. Bring to boil over medium heat.
3. Reduce heat and simmer for 2 minutes.
4. Remove saucepan from heat and puree the soup using a blender until smooth.
5. Stir in pesto, dried basil, vinegar, and erythritol.
6. Stir well and serve warm.

Nutrition: Calories: 662 Carbs: 18g Protein: 8g Fat: 55g

Basil Tomato Soup

Preparation Time: 10 minutes
Cooking Time: 10 minutes

Vegan Mushroom Bean Burger

Preparation Time: 10 mins
Cooking Time: 10 mins
Servings: 4
Ingredients:

- 3 tablespoon of canola oil (divided; or vegetable oil)
- 1 small onion (white or yellow, diced)
- 1 clove garlic (minced)
- 3/4 cup of mushrooms (fresh, diced small)
- 3 green onions (diced)
- 1/2 teaspoon of cumin
- 2 tablespoons of warm water
- 1 1/2 teaspoons of egg replacer
- 1 (15-ounce) can of pinto beans
- 1 teaspoon of fresh parsley (minced)
- Salt (to taste)
- Black pepper (to taste)

Direction:

1. Over medium heat, add the oil to a skillet.
2. Saute the diced garlic and onion in 1 tablespoon of canola oil, until the onions are soft, for about 5 minutes.
3. Add the green onions, chopped mushrooms, and cumin and cook until mushrooms are cooked, for about 5 minutes.
4. You can add extra oil if you want.
5. Set the mushroom and cooked onion mixture aside.
6. Combine the egg replacer and warm water in a small bowl, and mix together.
7. It will act as your binding agent.
8. Mash the beans until well mashed, using a potato masher or fork.
9. You can also pulse them in a food processor if you want.
10. Add the egg replacer mixture.
11. Stir until thoroughly combined.
12. Combine the mashed beans mixture with the mushroom and onion mixture and add the salt, parsley, with pepper in a large bowl.
13. Make sure the ingredients are well combined.
14. Shape mixture into patties (about 1-inch thick).
15. In a skillet over medium heat, heat the rest of the oil and cook for about 3 minutes on

each side, until the veggies burgers are done.

16. Serve with your favorite toppings, and enjoy.

Nutrition: Calories: 313cal | Fat: 4g | Protein: 18g | Fiber: 15g | Sodium: 107mg | Calcium: 172mg | Sugar: 0g | Carbohydrate: 55g

Grilled Stuffed Chili Rellenos

Preparation Time: 15 mins
Cooking Time: 45 mins
Servings: 6
Ingredients:
- 6 large poblano chiles or green bell peppers
- 2 tablespoons of olive oil
- 1 teaspoon of ground cumin
- 1 28 ounces can of vegetarian baked beans, drained
- 1 to 3 teaspoons of hot sauce, to taste
- 12 ounces of Pepper Jack or Monterey Jack cheese, coarsely grated
- Salt, to taste
- Freshly ground black pepper, to taste
- 1 medium onion, finely chopped
- 2 cloves garlic, finely chopped
- 2 jalapenos, seeded and chopped
- 1/2 red bell pepper, finely chopped
- 1/2 cup of chopped fresh cilantro

Direction:
1. Cut poblano chiles into half lengthwise.
2. This will help create a boat for filling.
3. Scrape out the seeds.
4. In a nonstick skillet, heat 2 tablespoons of olive oil.
5. Add garlic, onion, red bell pepper, jalapenos, cumin, and cilantro, and cook over medium heat for bout 4 minutes until golden brown.
6. Remove pan from the heat.
7. Stir in the baked beans, 8 ounces of cheese, and hot sauce.
8. Add a bit of pepper and salt to taste.
9. Spoon the mixture into the hollowed chiles, then sprinkle with the rest of the cheese.
10. Set up your grill for indirect grilling.

11. Preheat to medium and arrange the chilies on the grill away from the direct heat.
12. Cook until cheese is browned, and chilies are tender and bubbling for about 30 to 40 minutes.
13. Remove from grill, serve and enjoy.

Nutrition: Calories: 774cal | Fat: 24g | Protein: 46g | Fiber: 28g | Sodium: 461mg | Calcium: 730mg | Carb: 98g

Spinach Quinoa Lasagna Casserole

Preparation Time: 10 mins
Cooking Time: 60 mins
Servings: 6
Ingredients:

- 1,5 cups of truRoots Organic Sprouted Quinoa
- 1/2 medium yellow onion, finely diced
- 2,5 cups of bella mushrooms, diced
- 4 cups of spinach, fresh Marinara Mixture:
- 1 cup of ricotta cheese, full-fat
- 1 tablespoon of Italian seasoning
- 2 teaspoons of garlic powder
- 1/8 teaspoon of sea salt
- 2 cups of organic marinara sauce
- 2,5 cups of vegetable broth
- 1 cup of 1% cottage cheese
- 1/8 teaspoon of ground pepper For the Top:
- 1,5 cups of shredded mozzarella

4 medium tomatoes, sliced
Direction
1. Preheat oven to 375 degrees f and use coconut oil cooking spray to spray your casserole dish.
2. Prep veggies by chopping the mushrooms and dicing the onions.
3. Place the veggies with the spinach into the greased casserole dish.
4. Add truRoots Whole Grain Sprouted Quinoa in the casserole dish, and set it aside.
5. Mix the ingredients for the marinara sauce together in a medium-size bowl.
6. Add the marinara mixture into the casserole dish.

7. Mix all ingredients together by using a large spoon, making sure everything is covered.
8. Cover with tin foil.
9. Bake for about 30-mins; then, remove and stir.
10. Place it back inside the oven for 30 minutes, but covered.
11. Remove, and add mozzarella and sliced tomatoes to the top, then place it back in the oven for about 2 minutes.
12. Remove, then let it cool just before serving, for about 10 minutes.
13. Serve with fresh basil and a glass of red wine.
14. Enjoy.

Nutrition: Calories: 401cal | Fat: 15g | Protein: 22g | Fiber: 6g | Sugar: 45g | Carb: 10g

Vegan Pumpkin Risotto

Preparation Time: 10 mins
Cooking Time: 25 mins
Servings: 4 to 6
Ingredients
- 1 cup of canned pumpkin
- 1 teaspoon of fresh ginger (grated or minced)
- 1 teaspoon of nutmeg
- 1 tablespoon of fresh basil (chopped)
- 1 onion (diced)
- 1 tablespoon of olive oil
- 2 cups of arborio (risotto) rice
- 1 cup of white wine
- 4 cups of vegetable broth
- 1 tablespoon of vegan margarine or butter
- Salt and pepper, to taste

Direction
1. Over medium heat, saute the onions in the olive oil until the onion is mostly soft, for about 3 to 5 minutes.
2. Add in the rice.
3. Allow to cook for 1 - 2 minutes, stirring, just lightly toast the rice and be careful it doesn't burn.
4. Add in the white wine slowly.
5. Add half cup of vegetable broth at a time.
6. Allow the moisture to cook off just before adding the next 1/2 cup.
7. Stir frequently, and go ahead with adding the vegetable broth 1/2 cup at a time.

8. Add the rice that is nearly cooked once you've added all the vegetable broth, add in the nutmeg, fresh ginger, pumpkin, fresh basil, and vegan butter or margarine.
9. Stir everything well to combine, and season with a bit of pepper and salt lightly, to taste.
10. Heat everything just for another 1 - 2 minutes, frequently stirring until everything is heated through thoroughly.
11. Serve and enjoy.

Nutrition: Calories: 329cal | Fat: 4g | Protein: 7g | Fiber: 3g | Sodium: 550mg | Calcium: 51mg | Sugar: 0g | Carbohydrate: 58g

Couscous Stuffed Bell Peppers

Preparation Time: 15 mins
Cooking Time: 35 mins
Servings: 6
Ingredients:
- 4 to 6 green onions (scallions, sliced)
- 2 tablespoons of fresh lemon juice
- 2 tablespoons of olive oil
- 1/4 cup of fresh parsley (chopped)
- 1/2 cup of couscous (uncooked)
- 1 cup of water
- 6 whole bell peppers (any color)
- 2 red or yellow bell peppers (diced)
- salt and pepper to taste

Direction:
1. Place 1 cup of water in a medium-sized saucepan.
2. Then bring water to boil.
3. Add in the couscous once the water is boiling, and give it a quick stir.
4. Cover the pan.
5. Turn off the heat and then allow the couscous to sit for about 10 minutes, or until the couscous becomes fluffy when stirred with a fork.
6. Allow the couscous to cool completely.
7. Preheat oven to 350 degrees f. Slice the stems while your couscous is cooling or sitting, and tops off the whole bell peppers.

8. Then remove the seeds and cores carefully from the inside of each bell pepper.
9. Combine the cooled couscous, the sliced green onions, with the diced bell peppers in a large bowl.
10. Whisk the lemon juice, chopped fresh parsley, and olive oil together in a separate small bowl until well combined.
11. Pour this dressing over the couscous mixture.
12. Toss to combine gently.
13. Spoon the couscous into each whole green bell pepper.
14. Sprinkle pepper and salt on top.
15. In a preheated oven, roast the stuffed bell peppers until your bell peppers are tender or for about 35 minutes.
16. Serve and enjoy.

Nutrition: Calories: 151cal | Fat: 5g | Protein: 4g | Fiber: 5g | Sodium: 65mg | Calcium: 41mg | Sugar: 0g | Carbohydrate: 23g

Black Bean and Quinoa Stew

Preparation time: 10 minutes
Cooking time: 6 hours
Servings: 6
Ingredients:
- 1-pound black beans, dried, soaked overnight
- 3/4 cup quinoa, uncooked
- 1 medium red bell pepper, cored, chopped
- 1 medium red onion, peeled, diced
- 1 medium green bell pepper, cored, chopped
- 28-ounce diced tomatoes
- 2 dried chipotle peppers
- 1 ½ teaspoon minced garlic
- 2/3 teaspoon sea salt
- 2 teaspoons red chili powder
- 1/3 teaspoon ground black pepper
- 1 teaspoon coriander powder
- 1 dried cinnamon stick
- 1/4 cup cilantro
- 7 cups of water

Directions:
1. Switch on the slow cooker, add all the ingredients in it, except for salt, and stir until mixed.

2. Shut the cooker with lid and cook for 6 hours at a high heat setting until cooked.
3. When done, stir salt into the stew until mixed, remove cinnamon sticks and serve.

Nutrition: Calories: 308Kcal; Fat: 2g; Carbs: 70g; Fiber: 32g; Protein: 23g

Root Vegetable Stew

Preparation time: 10 minutes
Cooking time: 8 hours and 10 minutes
Servings: 6
Ingredients:
- 2 cups chopped kale
- 1 large white onion, peeled, chopped
- 1-pound parsnips, peeled, chopped
- 1-pound potatoes, peeled, chopped
- 2 celery ribs, chopped
- 1-pound butternut squash, peeled, deseeded, chopped
- 1-pound carrots, peeled, chopped
- 3 teaspoons minced garlic
- 1-pound sweet potatoes, peeled, chopped
- 1 bay leaf
- 1 teaspoon ground black pepper
- 1/2 teaspoon sea salt
- 1 tablespoon chopped sage
- 3 cups vegetable broth

Directions:
1. Switch on the slow cooker, add all the ingredients in it, except for the kale, and stir until mixed.
2. Shut the cooker with lid and cook for 8 hours at a low heat setting until cooked.
3. When done, add kale into the stew, stir until mixed, and cook for 10 minutes until leaves have wilted.
4. Serve straight away.

Nutrition: Calories: 120Kcal; Fat: 1g; Carbs: 28g; Fiber: 6g; Protein: 4g

Bean and Mushroom Chili

Preparation time: 15 minutes
Cooking time: 38 minutes
Servings: 6
Ingredients:

- 1 large onion, peeled and chopped
- 1-pound (454 g) button mushrooms, chopped
- 6 cloves garlic, peeled and minced
- 1 tablespoon ground cumin
- 4 teaspoons ground fennel
- 1 tablespoon ancho chile powder
- ½ teaspoon cayenne pepper
- 1 tablespoon unsweetened cocoa powder
- 4 cups cooked pinto beans, drained and rinsed
- 1 (28-ounce / 794-g) can diced tomatoes
- Salt, to taste (optional)

Directions:
1. Put the mushrooms and onion in a saucepan and sauté over medium heat for 10 minutes.
2. Add the garlic, cumin, fennel, chile powder, cayenne pepper, and cocoa powder and cook for 3 minutes.
3. Add the beans, tomatoes, and 2 cups of water and simmer, covered, for 25 minutes.
4. Season with salt, if desired.
5. Serve immediately.

Nutrition: Calories: 436Kcal; Fat: 2g; Carbs: 97g; Fiber: 23g; Protein: 19g

Five-Bean Chili

Preparation time: 10 minutes
Cooking time: 1 hour
Servings: 8
Ingredients:
- 2 (26- to 28-ounce / 737- to 794-g) cans diced tomatoes
- 1 (19-ounce / 539-g) can red kidney beans, drained and rinsed
- 1 (19-ounce / 539-g) can white kidney beans, drained and rinsed
- 1 (19-ounce / 539-g) can chickpeas, drained and rinsed
- 1 (19-ounce / 539-g) can black beans, drained and rinsed
- 1 (19-ounce / 539-g) can pinto beans, drained and rinsed
- 2 1/2 cups fresh mushrooms, sliced 1 medium red bell pepper, chopped
- 1 large yellow onion, chopped
- 1 cup corn, canned or frozen
- 1½ tablespoons chili powder

- 1 teaspoon ground cumin
- ½ teaspoon freshly ground black pepper
- ½ teaspoon pink Himalayan salt
- ¼ teaspoon cayenne pepper
- ¼ teaspoon garlic powder

Directions:

1. Combine all the ingredients in a large pot over medium heat.
2. Cover the pot with a lid and cook, stirring occasionally, for 45 to 60 minutes.
3. Serve as is, or on a bed of brown rice, quinoa, or with a fresh avocado.
4. If you have leftovers or you're doing meal prep, store in reusable containers in the refrigerator for up to 5 days or freeze for up to 2 months.

Nutrition: Calories: 756Kcal; Fat: 5g; Carbs: 139g; Fiber: 41g; Protein: 41g

Mushroom & Wild Rice Stew

Preparation time: 10 minutes
Cooking time: 50 minutes

Servings: 6
Ingredients:

- 1 to 2 teaspoons olive oil
- 2 cups chopped mushrooms
- ½ to 1 teaspoon salt
- 1 onion, chopped, or 1 teaspoon onion powder
- 3 or 4 garlic cloves, minced, or ½ teaspoon garlic powder
- 1 tablespoon dried herbs
- ¾ cup brown rice
- ¼ cup wild rice or additional brown rice
- 3 cups water
- 3 Vegetable Broth or store-bought broth
- 2 to 4 tablespoons balsamic vinegar (optional)
- Freshly ground black pepper
- 1 cup frozen peas, thawed
- 1 cup unsweetened nondairy milk (optional)
- 1 to 2 cups chopped greens, such as spinach, kale, or chard

Directions:

1. Heat the olive oil in a large soup pot over medium-high heat.
2. Add the mushrooms and a pinch of salt, and sauté for about 4 minutes, until the mushrooms are softened.

3. Add the onion and garlic (if using fresh), and sauté for 1 to 2 minutes more.
4. Stir in the dried herbs (plus the onion powder and/or garlic powder, if using), white or brown rice, wild rice, water, vegetable broth, vinegar (if using), and salt and pepper to taste.
5. Bring to a boil, turn the heat to low, and cover the pot.
6. Simmer the soup for 15 minutes (for white rice) or 45 minutes (for brown rice).
7. Turn off the heat and stir in the peas, milk (if using), and greens.
8. Let the greens wilt before serving.
9. Leftovers will keep in an airtight container for up to 1 week in the refrigerator or up to 1 month in the freezer.

Nutrition: Calories: 201Kcal; Fat: 3g; Carbs: 44g; Fiber: 4g; Protein: 6g

Dessert

Zesty Orange-Cranberry Energy Bites

Preparation time: 10 minutes

Cooking time: 0 minutes

Servings: 12

Ingredients:

- 2 tablespoons almond butter, or cashew or sunflower seed butter
- 2 tablespoons maple syrup or brown rice syrup
- 3/4 cup cooked quinoa
- 1/4 cup sesame seeds, toasted
- 1 tablespoon chia seeds
- ½ teaspoon almond extract, or vanilla extract Zest of 1 orange
- 1 tablespoon dried cranberries
- ¼ cup ground almonds

Directions:

1   In a medium bowl, mix the nut or seed butter and syrup until smooth and creamy.

2   Stir in the rest of the ingredients, and mix to make sure the consistency is holding together in a ball.

3   Form the mix into 12 balls.

4   Place them on a baking sheet lined with parchment or waxed paper and put them in the fridge to set for about 15 minutes.

5   If your balls aren't holding together, it's likely because of the moisture content of your cooked quinoa.

6   Add more nut or seed butter mixed with syrup until it all sticks together.

Nutrition: Calories: 109Kcal; Fat: 7g; Carbs: 11g; Fiber: 3g; Protein: 3g

Chocolate and Walnut Farfalle

Preparation time: 10 minutes
Cooking time: 0 minutes
Servings: 4
Ingredients:

- 1/2 cup chopped toasted walnuts
- 1/4 cup vegan semisweet chocolate pieces
- ounces farfalle
- 3 tablespoons vegan margarine
- 1/4 cup light brown sugar

Directions:

1 In a food processor or blender, grind the walnuts and chocolate pieces until crumbly.
2 Do not over-process.
3 Set aside. In a pot of boiling salted water, cook the farfalle, stirring occasionally, until al dente, about 8 minutes.
4 Drain well and return to the pot.
5 Add the margarine and sugar and toss to combine and melt the margarine.
6 Transfer the noodle mixture to a serving

Nutrition: Calories: 81Kcal; Fat: 37.64g; Carbs: 42.38g; Fiber: 4.8 g; Protein: 8.68g

Almond-Date Energy Bites

Preparation time: 5 minutes
Servings: 24
Ingredients:

- 1 cup dates, pitted
- 1 cup unsweetened shredded coconut

- ¼ cup chia seeds
- ¾ cup ground almonds
- ¼ cup cocoa nibs, or non-dairy chocolate chips

Directions:

1 Purée everything in a food processor until crumbly and sticking together, pushing down the sides whenever necessary to keep it blending.

2 If you don't have a food processor, you can mash soft medjool dates.

3 But if you're using harder baking dates, you'll have to soak them and then try to purée them in a blender.

4 Form the mix into 24 balls and place them on a baking sheet lined with parchment or waxed paper.

5 Put in the fridge to set for about 15 minutes.

6 Use the softest dates you can find.

7 Medjool dates are the best for this purpose.

8 The hard dates you see in the baking aisle of your supermarket are going to take a long time to blend up.

9 If you use those, try soaking them in water for at least an hour before you start and then draining.

Nutrition: Calories: 152Kcal; Fat: 11g; Carbs: 13g; Fiber: 5g; Protein: 3g

Pumpkin Pie Cups

Preparation time: 5 minutes
Cooking time: 6 minutes
Servings: 4-6
Ingredients:

- 1 cup canned pumpkin purée
- 1 cup nondairy milk

- tablespoons unrefined sugar or pure maple syrup (less if using sweetened milk), plus more for sprinkling
- ¼ cup spelt flour or all-purpose flour
- ½ teaspoon pumpkin pie spice
- Pinch salt

Directions:

1. Preparing the ingredients.
2. In a medium bowl, stir together the pumpkin, milk, sugar, flour, pumpkin pie spice, and salt.
3. Pour the mixture into 4 heat-proof ramekins.
4. Sprinkle a bit more sugar on the top of each, if you like.
5. Put a trivet in the bottom of your electric pressure cooker's cooking pot and pour in a cup or two of water.
6. Place the ramekins onto the trivet, stacking them if needed (3 on the bottom, 1 on top). High pressure for 6 minutes.
7. Close and lock the lid and ensure the pressure valve is sealed, then select high pressure and set the time for 6 minutes.
8. Pressure release.
9. Once the cooking time is complete, quick release the pressure, being careful not to get your fingers or face near the steam release.
10. Once all the pressure has been released, carefully unlock and remove the lid.
11. Let cool for a few minutes before carefully lifting out the ramekins with oven mitts or tongs.
12. Let cool for at least 10 minutes before serving.

Nutrition: Calories: 129Kcal; Fat: 1g; Carbs: 28g; Fiber: 3g; Protein: 3g

Granola-Stuffed Baked Apples

Preparation time: 10 minutes
Cooking time: 60 minutes
Servings: 4
Ingredients:

- 1/2 cup vegan granola, homemade or store-bought
- 2 tablespoons creamy peanut butter or almond butter
- 1 tablespoon vegan margarine
- 1 tablespoon pure maple syrup
- 1/2 teaspoon ground cinnamon
- 4 granny smith or other firm baking apples
- 1 cup apple juice

Directions:

1. Preheat the oven to 350°f. Grease a 9 x 13-inch baking pan and set it aside.
2. In a medium bowl, combine the granola, peanut butter, margarine, maple syrup, and cinnamon and mix well.
3. Core the apples and stuff the granola mixture into the centers of the apples, packing tightly.
4. Place the apples upright in the prepared pan.
5. Pour the apple juice over the apples and bake until tender, about 1 hour.
6. Serve warm.

Nutrition: Calories: 361Kcal; Fat: 13.65g; Carbs: 60.8g; Fiber: 8.4g; Protein: 7.65g

Black Bean Brownie Pops

Preparation time: 45 minutes

Cooking time: 2 minutes

Servings: 12

Ingredients:

- 3/4 cup chocolate chips
- ounce cooked black beans
- 1 tablespoon maple syrup
- tablespoons cacao powder
- 1/8 teaspoon sea salt
- tablespoons sunflower seed butter

Directions:

1. Place black beans in a food processor, add remaining ingredients, except for chocolate, and pulse for 2 minutes until combined and the dough starts to come together.
2. Shape the dough into twelve balls, arrange them on a baking sheet lined with parchment paper, then insert a toothpick into each ball and refrigerate for 20 minutes.
3. Then meat chocolate in the microwave for 2 minutes, and dip brownie pops in it until covered.
4. Return the pops into the refrigerator for 10 minutes until set and then serve

Nutrition: Calories: 218Kcal; Fat: 20g; Carbs: 7.1g; Protein: 1.5g

Peppermint Oreos

Preparation time: 2 hours

Cooking time: 0 minute

Servings: 12

Ingredients:

For the Cookies:

- 1 cup dates
- 2/3 cup brazil nuts
- tablespoons carob powder
- 2/3 cup almonds
- 1/8 teaspoon sea salt
- tablespoons water

For the Crème:

- tablespoons almond butter
- 1 cup coconut chips
- tablespoons melted coconut oil
- 1 cup coconut shreds
- drops of peppermint oil
- 1/2 teaspoon vanilla powder

For the Dark Chocolate:

- 3/4 cup cacao powder
- 1/2 cup date paste
- 1/3 cup coconut oil, melted

Directions:

1. Prepare the cookies, and for this, place all its ingredients in a food processor and pulse for 3 to 5 minutes until the dough comes together.

2. Then place the dough between two parchment sheets, roll the dough, then cut out twenty-four cookies of the desired shape and freeze until solid.

3. Prepare the crème, and for this, place all its ingredients in a food processor and pulse for 2 minutes until smooth.

4. When cookies have harden, sandwich crème in between the cookies by placing dollops on top of a cookie and then pressing it with another cookie.

5. Freeze the cookies for 30 minutes and in the meantime, prepare chocolate and for this, place all its ingredients in a bowl and whisk until combined.

6. Dip frouncesen cookie sandwich into chocolate, at least two times, and then

freeze for another 30 minutes until chocolate has hardened.

7 Serve straight away.

Nutrition: Calories: 301Kcal; Fat: 21g; Carbs: 9g; Protein: 1.9g

Snickers Pie

Preparation time: 4 hours
Cooking time: 0 minute
Servings: 16
Ingredients:
For the Crust:

- Medjool dates, pitted
- 1 cup dried coconut, unsweetened
- tablespoons cocoa powder
- 1/2 teaspoon sea salt
- 1 teaspoon vanilla extract, unsweetened
- 1 cup almonds

For the Caramel Layer:

- Medjool dates, pitted, soaked for 10 minutes in warm water, drained
- teaspoons vanilla extract, unsweetened
- teaspoons coconut oil
- tablespoons almond butter, unsalted

For the Peanut Butter Mousse:

- 3/4 cup peanut butter
- tablespoons maple syrup
- 1/2 teaspoon vanilla extract, unsweetened
- 1/8 teaspoon sea salt
- 28 ounces coconut milk, chilled

Directions:

1. Prepare the crust, and for this, place all its ingredients in a food processor and pulse for 3 to 5 minutes until the thick paste comes together.
2. Take a baking pan, line it with parchment paper, place

crust mixture in it and spread and press the mixture evenly in the bottom, and freeze until required.

3. Prepare the caramel layer, and for this, place all its ingredients in a food processor and pulse for 2 minutes until smooth.

4. Pour the caramel on top of the prepared crust, smooth the top and freeze for 30 minutes until set.

5. Prepare the mousse and for this, separate coconut milk and its solid, then add solid from coconut milk into a food processor, add remaining ingredients and then pulse for 1 minute until smooth.

6. Top prepared mousse over caramel layer, and then freeze for 3 hours until set.

7. Serve straight away.

Nutrition: Calories: 311Kcal; Fat: 23g; Carbs: 9g; Protein: 1.9g

Peanut Butter Fudge

Preparation Time: 50 minutes
Cooking time: 1 minute
Servings: 8
Ingredients:

- 1/2 cup peanut butter
- tablespoons maple syrup
- 1/4 teaspoon salt
- tablespoons coconut oil, melted
- 1/4 teaspoon vanilla extract, unsweetened

Direction:

1 Take a heat-resistant bowl, place your entire shopping list: microwave for 15 seconds

in it, then stir until well combined.

2 Take a freezer-safe container, line it with parchment paper, pour in the fondant mixture, spread evenly and freeze for 40 minutes until solid and hard.

3 When ready to eat, let it rest for 5 minutes, then cut into squares and serve.

Nutrition: Calories: 96 Cal Fat: 3.6 g Carbs: 14.6 g Protein: 1.5 g Fiber: 0.3 g

Whipped Cream

Preparation Time: 5 Minutes
Cooking Time: 0 Minutes
Servings: 2
Ingredients:

- ¼ cup powdered sugar
- One teaspoon vanilla extract, unsweetened
- ounces coconut milk, unsweetened, chilled

Direction:

1. Take a bowl, leave it to cool overnight in the freezer, separate the coconut milk and the solid and add the solid from the coconut milk to the cold bowl.

2. Add the remaining shopping list: and beat everything for 3 minutes until smooth and well blended.

3. Serve immediately.

Nutrition: Calories: 40.4 Cal Fat: 1 g Carbs: 8 g Protein: 0 g Fiber: 0 g

Blueberry Mousse

Nutrition: Calories: 433 Cal Fat: 32.3 g Carbs: 44 g Protein: 5.1 g Fiber: 0 g

Preparation Time: 20 Minutes

Cooking Time: 0 Minutes

Servings: 2

Ingredients:

- 1 cup wild blueberries
- 1 cup cashews, soaked for 10 minutes, drained
- 1/2 teaspoon berry powder
- Two tablespoons coconut oil, melted
- One tablespoon lemon juice
- One teaspoon vanilla extract, unsweetened
- 1/4 cup hot water

Direction:

1 Mix the whole shopping list: in a food processor and work for 2 minutes until smooth.
2 Set aside until needed.

Brownie Batter

Preparation Time: 5 Minutes

Cooking Time: 0 Minutes

Servings: 4

Ingredients:

- Medjool dates, pitted, soaked in warm water
- 1,5 ounces chocolate, unsweetened, melted
- Two tablespoons maple syrup
- Four tablespoons tahini
- ½ teaspoon vanilla extract, unsweetened
- One tablespoon cocoa powder, unsweetened
- 1/8 teaspoon sea salt
- 1/8 teaspoon espresso powder

- to 4 tablespoons almond milk, unsweetened

Direction:

1. Combine all the Shopping List: use a food processor and process for 2 minutes until combined.
2. Set aside until required.

Nutrition: Calories: 44 Cal Fat: 1 g Carbs: 6 g Protein: 2 g Fiber: 0 g

Peanut Butter Bars

Preparation Time: 5 hours and 15 minutes

Cooking time: 5 minutes

Servings: 16

Ingredients:

- 1/2 cup cranberries
- Medjool dates, pitted
- 1 cup roasted almond
- 1 tablespoon chia seeds
- 1 1/2 cups oats
- 1/8 teaspoon salt
- 1/4 cup and 1 tablespoon agave nectar
- 1/2 teaspoon vanilla extract, unsweetened
- 1/3 cup and 1 tablespoon peanut butter, unsalted
- tablespoons water

Direction:

1. Place an almond in a food processor, blend until chopped and transfer it to a large bowl. Add the dates in the food processor along with the oats, pour in the water and the pulse for the dates is chopped.
2. Add the date mixture to the almond mixture, add the chia seeds and berries and mix until combined.
3. Take a saucepan, put it on medium heat, add the

remaining butter and the remaining shopping list:, stir and cook for 5 minutes until the mixture reaches a liquid consistency. Pour the butter mixture over the date mixture, then stir until well combined.

4 Take an 8 x 8 inch baking sheet, line it with parchment paper, add the date mixture, roll it out and press it evenly and refrigerate for 5 hours.

5 Cut it into sixteen bars and serve.

Nutrition: Calories: 187 Cal Fat: 7.5 g Carbs: 27.2 g Protein: 4.7 g Fiber: 2 g

Strawberry Mousse

Preparation Time: 5 Minutes
Cooking Time: 15 Minutes
Servings: 4

Ingredients:

- ounces coconut milk, unsweetened
- Two tablespoons honey
- Five strawberries

Direction:

1 Put the berries in a blender and blend until smooth.

2 Put the milk in a bowl, whisk until whipped, then add the remaining shopping list: and mix until well blended.

3 Refrigerate the mousse for 10 minutes and then serve.

Nutrition: Calories: 145 Cal Fat: 23 g Carbs: 15 g Protein: 5 g Fiber: 1 g

Choco-Cookies

Preparation Time: 40 minutes
Cooking time: 5 minutes
Servings: 4

Ingredients:

- 1/2 cup coconut oil
- 1 cup agave syrup
- 1/2 cup cocoa powder
- 1/2 teaspoon salt
- cups peanuts, chopped
- 1 cup peanut butter
- cups sunflower seeds

Nutrition: Calories: 148 Cal Fat: 7.4 g Carbs: 20 g Protein: 1.5 g Fiber: 0.6 g

Direction:

1 Take a small saucepan, put it on medium heat, add the first three shopping lists: and cook for 3 minutes until melted.

2 Boil the mixture for 1 minute, then remove the pan from the heat and mix with salt and butter until smooth.

3 Incorporate nuts and seeds until blended, then drop the mixture in the form of molds onto the baking sheet lined with wax paper and refrigerate for 30 minutes.

4 Serve immediately.

Conclusion

What are the health benefits of a vegetarian diet?

There is a large burden of disease in the Western world, but some foods have protective effects.

Adopting a vegetarian diet has many positive health effects, and by definition will encourage you to eat more of these protective vegetarian foods.

There are several vegetarian foods that are true health superstars, particularly for their cardiovascular protective properties. These include berries, green leafy vegetables and broccoli.

Legumes like beans and lentils are also phenomenal additions to the diet.

In addition to having a really healthy nutritional profile, they are an especially good carbohydrate swap and a good natural alternative to refined carbohydrates, which can cause harmful spikes in blood sugar, leading to weight gain, high blood pressure and high cholesterol.

Also, eating a vegetarian diet generally means you're eating a high-fiber diet compared to the average modern diet, which tends not to contain enough.

What are the disadvantages of a vegetarian diet?

Vegans are more at risk for nutrient deficiencies and need to be more careful about their eating habits.

When you eat animal products, the animal has done the hard work for you, and the nutrient dense profile has been built with relatively little work required by you to access this diverse range of nutrients.

Eating animal-based foods allows you to be a little lazier, but vegans need to be much more aware of what they are eating.

Is the vegetarian diet right for me?

As with all diets, most people find it difficult to maintain restrictive eating habits that go against their natural eating habits.

It has to be something you enjoy and a part of your lifestyle. Think long term rather than just short term.

Remember, cutting out all animal products is a big change in your diet and you should discuss it with your doctor before moving forward.